1970

99

THE SATIRE OF SAKI

"The satire should be like the porcupine
That shoots sharp quills out in each angry line."

JOSEPH HALL
First English satirist
(1574–1656)

THE SATIRE OF SAKI

A Study of the Satiric Art of
HECTOR H. MUNRO

BY

George James Spears

An Exposition–University Book

EXPOSITION PRESS   NEW YORK

EXPOSITION PRESS INC., 386 Park Avenue South, New York 16

FIRST EDITION

EP 41140

To the memory of

MY FATHER

ACKNOWLEDGMENT

SO MANY persons are involved in writing a study of this sort that one does not know where to begin in thanking them. Were I to express my gratitude to all those wonderful people, librarians where I have studied and taught, this volume would be much larger. Suffice to say I envy them their profession and attest that they have all been uniformly kind to me, particularly those at Russell Sage College and The New York State Library at Albany.

The guidance of Dr. Emmett O'Grady and the Reverend Raymond Shevenell, O.M.I., of the University of Ottawa, is reflected in the worth-while portions. Those open to criticism should be laid entirely at my door.

The encouragement and assistance of my wife, members of my office staff, and Dr. Virginia L. Radley, chairman of English at Sage, are appreciated more than I acknowledge from day to day. Without the generosity of President Lewis A. Froman of Russell Sage College this study would never have been written or published.

G. J. S.

Russell Sage College
Albany, New York
1963

CONTENTS

Introduction

THE relation of wit and humor to emotional expression, to the fine arts, and to the particular literary form in which it may appear, is well worth study. But the very conditions that would make such study interesting would demand an enormous accumulation of material and the strongest possible basis of scholarship and intellectual insight. The study of the satiric aspects of one author's art is a more modest task.

Satire, because of its large dependence on temporary or local conditions, is of all forms of literature one of the most ephemeral. Differences of interpretation exist among the authorities and show themselves particularly in the common usage of terms. Someone has remarked that everyone recognizes satire but no one can define it.

In his *Origin and Progress of Satire* Dryden emphasizes certain principles or canons of satire, particularly restraint and judgment, knowing not only when and where to strike but also how deep should be the thrust.[1]

The 1949 *Encyclopaedia Britannica* article on satire stresses the distinctly recognizable element of humor if the utterance is invested with literary form. Dr. Richard Garnett, who wrote the article, adds that satire must be honest, weighty, and durable.

Duffy's modern *Dictionary* describes satire as "a literary presentation of ridiculous aspects of an idea, person or kind of

---

1 Quoted in Raymond M. Alden, *Rise of Formal Satire in England*, p. 2.

behaviour with a view to correction," literally, "A dish of mixed foods."[2]

Alden insists satire must focus our gaze sharply upon the contrast between things as they should be and as they are. It must not cancel distortion with counter-distortion.[3] The great satirist sees straight, sees far, and sees deep. That is what makes him great.

Fowler's tabular statement on the nature of literary terms, as reproduced here, sheds valuable light on the relationship of literary distinctions.

	MOTIVE or AIM	PROVINCE	METHOD or MEANS	AUDIENCE
humour	Discovery	Human nature	Observation	The sympathetic
wit	Throwing light	Words & ideas	Surprise	The intelligent
satire	Amendment	Morals & manners	Accentuation	The self-satisfied
sarcasm	Inflicting pain	Faults & foibles	Inversion	Victim & bystander
invective	Discredit	Misconduct	Direct statement	The public
irony	Exclusiveness	Statement of facts	Mystification	An inner circle
cynicism	Self-justification	Morals	Exposure of nakedness	The respectable
The sardonic	Self-relief	Adversity	Pessimism	Self

For the purposes of this study satire shall be generally considered as the holding up to public ridicule in a distinctly literary manner the private vices and foibles of mankind for the purpose of correction and as a gesture of defiance.

The popularity and readability of that inimitable writer of fiction who began his literary career as a political satirist for the *Westminster Gazette* and, during 1902–1908, was correspondent in Russia and subsequently in Paris of the *Morning Post,* are well attested to by the countless enthusiastic and loyal champions of Saki. Unfortunately, however, although his readers are legion, his critics are few. And there can be little doubt that Chris-

---

[2] Charles Duffy and Henry Pettit, *A Dictionary of Literary Terms* (Denver, 1951), p. 88.

[3] Raymond M. Alden, *Rise of Formal Satire in England* (Philadelphia, 1899), p. 12.

topher Morley (in his introduction to the Viking edition of *The Short Stories of Saki—H. H. Munro*) is partially correct in saying that Saki should be read and enjoyed rather than dissected and analyzed. But to dismiss Saki as a mere entertainer and deprecate any critical analysis of his works is to by-pass wantonly one of the most efficacious and mordant artists the world has ever seen.

To be sure, the elusiveness of Saki's satiric humor may discourage analysis, but to appreciate fully and savor at leisure his trenchant irony and dry mockery is to experience at times the esthetic "shock of recognition" that one gets in poring over the works of such classics as Juvenal, Chaucer, Cervantes, Johnson, Molière, La Fontaine, Wycherley, Dryden, Pope, Congreve, Swift, Gay, Voltaire, Sterne, Byron, Dickens, Thackeray, Twain, and Sinclair Lewis, Aldous Huxley, Ring Lardner, and James Thurber in this century.

H. H. Munro's world puts one in mind of Restoration comedy and Oscar Wilde. It is a sophisticated world, marvelously attuned to and acquainted with the mockery of well-bred malice. Saki's wit is at once baroque, electric, and disarming. The glittering banter and repartee of his characters put one in mind of the deadly aphorism in which Pope's age was so adept. His depraved young men have an Iago-like cruelty seldom if ever distilled by the epicurean snobbery of Oscar Wilde's *dramatis personae*. Saki, in fact, often combines the Juvenalian *saeva indignatio* with the Horatian urbanity. He manages to undermine the pretentious hypocrisies and intrinsic follies of *Homo sapiens* without ever resorting to the vitriolic intellectual scorn or physical nausea of Swift. It is noteworthy that just as Swift utilizes a naïve, unsophisticated sailor, Lemuel Gulliver, to puncture the ridiculous ramifications of Man's PRIDE, Munro employs young children as his instruments of chastisement. Usually a precocious stripling is used to deflate and puncture an egoism more vulgar and infantile than his own; a six-year-old boy or a self-possessed young lady of nine inflicts a damaging blow to some adult pretension or foible.

The purpose of this thesis will be to analyze in some detail the art of Munro and to show how he wielded his satiric barbs in assailing human fatuity as well as social, intellectual snobbery. It will be shown that his envenomed darts are indiscriminately hurled at the dullness of upper-middle-class Englishmen, the unimaginative politicians, the emancipated sybarites, and the philistines of artistic literary fashions. The dominating female and the obtuse pedagogue will be found to be two of his favorite targets. Without too much straining, it will be comparatively easy to demonstrate that many of his animus-ridden stories are in a sense the wish fulfillment of a boy's dream. Saki, as a boy, suffered from some rather appalling aunts, so that again and again he shows childhood in cruel triumph over an adult. His terrifying children are legion and even Saki's mature men of the world have a touch of the *enfant terrible.*

The first chapter attempts to define Saki's position in the satiric tradition; the second is devoted to an examination of his short stories; the third and fourth chapters perform a similar service for his novels, plays, and political writings; and the conclusion seeks to evaluate and appraise the achievement or failure of Saki as a satirist.

THE SATIRE OF SAKI

CHAPTER I

The Satiric Tradition

The comical and painful are not objectively distinct. Every kind of humor can be matched by a kind of pain. Everything that is tragic may be comic if you contrive to take it playfully.—MAX EASTMAN

JUST AS it is by convention that the love lyrist treats of love, the elegist of grief, and the tragic dramatists of the most serious issues of life, so by convention the satirist concerns himself with vice and folly. Availing himself of the satiric spectrum (wit, ridicule, irony, sarcasm, cynicism, the sardonic, and invective), the satirist seeks to effect reform and correction by tilting at the windmills of human follies and foibles. Whether his mode of criticism be Horatian (the genial, laughing, urbane satire of Horace) or Juvenalian (the caustic, corrosive satire of Juvenal), his intent is ever one and the same: to expose and flay the vices, inanities, affectations, hypocrisies, and stupidities of man and his society. Even laughing satire is laughing at, not merely irresponsible laughing. It invites us not to let down our hair and relax, but to lift our eyebrows and mock. The satirist is always aggressively on the offensive. He exposes pretension and strips away false fronts. His laughter is always spiced with something of malice. It is in the main a scornful amusement at the failings and shortcomings of an individual or of human nature and human institutions in general.

The great satirist has behind him the driving force of moral conviction, a burning hatred of evil. Even the hatred engendered from personal resentment is, if not a noble passion, nevertheless a very intense passion; and intensity is one of the elements of great literature. When the satirist looks on the multitude and is moved to Jovian wrath by its pettiness and iniquity, he cannot refrain from lashing out furiously and indignantly. Swift was a churchman who preached and practiced charity, but he was surrounded by yahoos who tore their weaker fellows limb from limb out of lust for the yellow metal. We who are perhaps conscious of the same discrepancy between the ideals which the mind of man has discovered and the diseases which are his biological heritage are content to shrug our shoulders and to regard the ideals as academic unrealities in an acquisitive society. Swift could not be so complacent. Unlike his lifelong friend Congreve, who saw the facts just as clearly, he did not settle down in the lap of a fat, doting duchess to eat chocolates at her expense. Swift's moral animus impelled him with a hunger meat and drink could not sate, and sent him away from afternoon teas out of love with superficial prattle.

An even more significant aspect of the truly great satiric artist is his adherence to the facts of life. Satire is an act of heightened realism—at its greatest, of a universalized realism. This is not to say, of course, that satire precludes the use of fancy and imagination—Pope's *The Rape of the Lock* would refute anyone so foolhardy as to maintain this. Yet it can be safely submitted that the satirist's appeal is primarily an intellectual rather than an emotional one. To write great satire requires a high degree of intellectual maturity. The satirist must be a master of perspective. But before he can attain to that mastery he must be able to see life steadily and see it whole.

Even comic satire derives its significance from its truth. And since the truth is frequently unpalatable to a benighted mankind, people have repeatedly averred that there is something unpleasant about satire. They resent the sneer in its laughter and their gorges rise at its uninhibited frankness. They righteously ask whether there is not a mental quirk behind the jaundiced vision which is the satirist's. And in part their protestation has a valid basis. For to the misogynistic and embittered Swift, to the ironical scrutiny of Anatole France, virtue was less visible than vice. But that is not to say that the vice which they oppugned was not real; we cannot deny it because it was almost all they saw. Satire is the indispensable antidote to the specious and fallacious panaceas of humankind. At its sanest and most penetrating it cuts through superficialities and attains to the naked vision of Blake. It focuses our gaze sharply upon the perennial dichotomy between appearance and reality. The satirist's is the inevitable logic of the empiricist intent on dispelling misconceptions and delusions. That is why the satirist flourishes best during periods of intellectual ferment, when iconoclasts are calling all in doubt.

Periclean Athens had the disarming mockery of Plato and the satiric genius of Aristophanes. Augustan Rome had the urbane wit of Horace; the seething Empire of the second century, Juvenal, Martial, and Lucan. The renascent Europe of the late Middle Ages had Boccaccio, Chaucer, and Langland. With the full bursting forth of the Renaissance came the great voices of Rabelais, Aretino, Cervantes, and all the wit and satire of Elizabethan drama. Modern European history has been fully represented by a multitude of literary artists who excelled in the genre of satire: Molière, Dryden, Pope, Swift, Fielding, Wycherley, Voltaire, Sterne, Burns, Byron, Dickens, and Thackeray.

The growth of commerce altered the face of the seventeenth-century world. The Industrial Revolution with its far-reaching technological developments, its precipitation of the shift from the country to the city, provided suitable and abundant grist for the satiric mills of nineteenth-century English littérateurs. Byron lashed the cant and hypocrisy of society by pointing an invidious comparison between the evils engendered by artificial, man-made conventions and the innate good of the natural. Blake and Peacock took exception to materialism. Thackeray launched memorable attacks against snobs and snobbery. Dickens inveighed violently against the social ills of his age. Nor was the spirit of satire dormant on the continent and in America, for, contributing to the general stream of rebuke and ridicule, there were Leopardi, Balzac, Flaubert, Ibsen, Mark Twain, Chekhov, Heine, Gogol, Anatole France, Marcel Proust.

What is more, the flood did not abate with the inception of the twentieth century. On the contrary, it continued to swell and reached Gargantuan proportions in the writings of H. G. Wells, George Bernard Shaw, Norman Douglas, Max Beerbohm, Thorstein Veblen, Ring Lardner, James Joyce, Sinclair Lewis, and Aldous Huxley. Even in those novelists who are not essentially satiric, there is a strong undercurrent of ironic depreciation of man's pretension as compared to his achievement. One has only to call to mind John Galsworthy, D. H. Lawrence, Ernest Hemingway, John Steinbeck, James T. Farrell, John Dos Passos, William Faulkner, and Thomas Wolfe to be reminded that the satiric imp is at play in many of their most distinguished pages. As for our avowed comic writers—Donald Ogden Stewart, James Thurber, Roy Campbell, Frank Sullivan, A. P. Herbert, Robert Benchley, to name only a few—they are more than two-thirds satirists. Even biography is tinged nowadays with satire as in the trenchant portraits of Lytton Strachey. And the same applies to modern poetry, from the esoteric involutions of T. S. Eliot's "Prufrock" to the lighthearted verbal gymnastics of Ogden Nash.

One thing then is clear: the satiric vein is in conspicuous prominence in the writings of our time. Modern satirists like Sinclair Lewis, W. H. Auden, Ezra Pound, Kenneth Fearing, Siegfried Sassoon, and Edith Sitwell call attention to contemporary confusion of thought and impress upon us anew the need for shaping order out of chaos. One of the most remarkable features of modern literature is the union of caricature with literature when it does not sink to mimicry. The present-day satirist analyzes keenly the fatuity of the social pattern and the personal neuroses developing therefrom. Much of the poetry of Roy Campbell, for example, puts us in mind of Swift, just as the satire of Kenneth Fearing against the middle class reminds us of Dickens and Thackeray. It is not at all too farfetched, in fact, to claim that if we ever become truly civilized and rid ourselves of our inveterate homicidal mania, satire will be found to have been a very efficacious agent in bringing about our return to sanity. For, as suggested above, the criteria of satire are, and always have been, truth and sanity; that, in a word, is the *raison d'être* of satire: to rescue man from the beasts and return him to the angels. That also constitutes the intrinsic worth of satire, which is always, at bottom, constructive and idealistic, and which always recoils from the counterfeit and the mean. The great satirist believes in the worth and dignity of man; his is an unstinting affirmation of life. That is what makes him great.

Is it, therefore, as a satirist that the true greatness of Hector Hugh Munro ("Saki")[1] can be appreciated? Although one of the most popular of popular short-story writers, Munro has

---

[1] H. H. Munro was born in Burma of Celtic descent in 1870. He was educated in England, and upon his father's retirement from foreign service traveled much in Europe. After a brilliant career in London as a journalist, he enlisted immediately upon England's declaration of war against Germany, and was killed in action in 1916 at Beaumont-Hamel.

He began writing fiction in 1896 under the pseudonym Saki, the name of the cupbearer in *The Rubaiyat of Omar Khayyam*. Between 1902 and 1908 he served as a British newspaper correspondent in the Balkans, Russia, and France. Most of his short stories were written after he had settled again in England. Beside his short stories, now collected into one volume, *The Complete Short Stories of Saki* (1930), he wrote several other works, including a novel, *The Unbearable Bassington* (1912), and a number of plays.

hitherto never served as the subject of a serious study. It has
been claimed that the elusive flavor of Saki's satire resists analysis[2] and that the exquisite lightness of his work offers no grasp
for the solemnities of earnest criticism.[3] But this is patently a
begging of the question as well as being beside the point. Saki
was not merely intent upon entertaining his readers; rather, like
Swift, he desired to vex them into an awareness of their follies.
His adeptness in the mockery of well-bred malice, his lively eye
for human frailties and the jibes of circumstance, his genius in
compressing into a short story an amazingly full and unsolemn
comment upon English Society—all these demand as well as
merit the scrutiny and analysis of a scholarly study. Few short-
story writers have wielded with more adroit mastery satire's
most effective weapon—irony. With the disarming nonchalance
and charm of an Oscar Wilde, Saki is forever exposing and
castigating the obtuseness, moral depravity, and barbarism that
festered underneath the surface polish and glitter of his own
orchidaceous milieu. In fact, there are few aspects of fatuity,
of esthetic philistinism, of social snobbery, of intellectual pretension, which are not sorely brought to task by Saki's satiric
barbs and poisoned darts.

> . . . a spirit of comfortable, even-tempered satire and philosophy,
> disclosing a mockery that did not trouble to be bitter, a joy in life
> that was not passionate to the verge of being troublesome.—H. H.
> MUNRO

Saki's range was narrow and he lacked variety, but in his own
field he was supreme and unique. The flavor of his wit cannot
be tasted vicariously. To convey any sense of its quality it will
be necessary to quote in detail the dazzling, malicious epigrams,
the wry, surprising twists of phrase, the cynical barbs of the
social satirist, which he tossed off so effortlessly and prolifically.

---

[2] Edgar Johnson, *A Treasury of Satire* (New York, 1945), p. 634.
[3] Christopher Morley, ed., *The Short Stories of Saki* (London, 1949), p. 5.

It is not the plots of his short stories that merit scrutiny—although Saki is, when he chooses, a master of trick endings, as in "Dusk" and "The Reticence of Lady Anne"—but rather the manner of his telling, the inimitable *sang-froid* that simultaneously disarms and pierces home. His mockery is urbane but at the same time ruthless. His satiric artillery is light but his aim is deadly; and humbug, hypocrisy, greed, envy, uncharitableness, dullness, and fatuity easily fall in the face of his withering barrage. Few other writers, in fact, demonstrate so forcibly that there is no just impediment to the marriage of wit and serious thought.

Like Dickens, Saki invented a world wholly his own. Except for an occasional peasant or shopkeeper with engaging oddities of character, the proletariat has no place in Saki's world. It is populated chiefly by elegant, impish young men with a fine taste for pranks and exotic food, by baroque baronesses and eccentric dukes, by flustered hostesses with unmanageable children, and by troublemakers of all breeds. And the settings of his stories are always the same: London parties and country week ends.

Certain types of characters and situations repeat themselves with paradoxically unwearying regularity. One is always, for example, met with unscrupulous and suave liars like the Reginalds and Clovises, who feed on plovers' eggs and aspic and who rid themselves of bores and disconcert the equanimity of prudes by devising all manner of ingenious pranks and hoaxes. Other prigs and Sir Fopling Flutters fall victim to the malevolent machinations and diablerie of those precociously shrewd and incorrigible children who appear to have been their inventor's pride and joy. Invariably we find a six-year-old boy or a self-possessed young lady of nine inflicting a mortal blow against the *amour-propre* of an adult.

The truth is that Saki himself has something of the inhuman

heartlessness of childhood. It was precisely this quality of his mind that S. P. B. Mais signaled out for pregnant comment. He wrote:

> Munro's understanding of children can only be explained by the fact that he was in many ways a child himself: his sketches betray a harshness, a love of practical jokes, a craze for animals of the most exotic breeds, a lack of mellow geniality that hint very strongly at the child in the man. Manhood has but placed in his hands a perfect sense of irony and withheld all other adult traits.
>
> In *The Mappined Life* we get for the first time near to the secret of a genius who did not unlock his heart. Here at last behind the child, the buffoon, the satirist, the eclectic, the aristocrat, the elegant man of the world, we can trace the features of one who discovered that the only way to make life bearable was to laugh at it.[4]

There can be little doubt that Mr. Mais overstates the case, but there is no mistaking a strain of cruelty in Saki, a quality of mind intrinsically akin to the unfeeling sadism of a child. Cleverness and insouciance almost always win out in his stories, which generally illustrate the maxim that our sweetest songs are those that tell of sadist (*sic!*) thought. Time and again he shows childhood in cruel triumph over an adult, playing on grownups some brilliant or brutal prank which is the wish fulfillment of a boy's dream. His terrifying children are legion. Clovis Sangrail and Bertie van Tahn, those seventeen-year-old terrors armed in insolence, unscrupulousness, and charm, are the exquisite projections of adolescent ambition. Even Saki's mature men of the world always have a touch of the *enfant terrible*. His esoteric flavor lies in this fusion of an elaborate and overpowering worldliness with boyhood brutality.

It is the constant ingredient of his wit. It appears in the mingled insouciance and rudeness of his incredible protagonists. It is present even in the consummate and surrealistic names he

---

[4] S. P. B. Mais, *Books and Their Writers* (New York, 1920), p. 329.

assigns to his characters: Sir Lulworth Quayne, Lady Greymartin, Ada Spelvexit, Leona Bimberton, and Mrs. Quabarl. Saki has no patience with stupid or stolid folk whom he condemns to grotesque mishaps with a grin of delighted malice. And yet only a moral zealot would be seriously exercised on such a score. For it is Saki's very malice which adds spice to his narratives.

His wit is in the tradition of Wilde and the lesser creations of E. F. Benson's *Dodo* and Anthony Hope's *Dolly Dialogues*. He has also affinities with Noel Coward and Aldous Huxley. Like them, he creates an artificial world enclosed in an element outside of which it could no more exist than we could exist outside our planetary atmosphere. And it is to an examination of this world that we now turn.

In the ensuing pages the short stories, novels, and dramas of Munro will be subjected to a careful analysis, with the intent of arriving at a clear understanding of the method, art, and content of this author's satire, if such it is.

CHAPTER II

The Short Stories

THE REGINALD SERIES

SAKI's first collection of short stories, collectively known as *Reginald,* comprises fifteen tales. The central figure in each is, of course, the blasé, modish man about town, Reginald, who alternately delights and antagonizes the reader by his infinite capacity for pungent raillery, sparkling *bon mots,* and cruel mockery. Many of the stories are really no more than discursive and fragmentary reflections on such routine topics of discussion as drama, war, conventions, tariffs, and religion. *Reginald* is by no means caviare to the general, and as one might suspect, it is here that we see Saki at his most ingenuous, most naïve, and most youthful.

The first story in the collection is a rather tame piece that recounts how Reginald disrupted the placid decorum of a garden party in high society by a variety of carefully calculated peccadilloes. He insults a highly esteemed colonel given to expansive boasting by rudely drawing attention to his senescence, teaches the younger Rampage boy the approved theory of mixing absinthe, within full earshot of his mother, who was prominent in a local temperance movement, discusses a risqué novel with the archdeacon's wife, and is hustled away by his friend only in time to prevent a complete fiasco.

"Reginald on Christmas Presents" is a trite comment on the exasperatingly uncanny predilection maiden aunts evince for giving atrocious Christmas gifts. Reginald's considered opinion is that the ideal yuletide present should consist of liqueurs or liqueur glasses and crystallized fruits. The attempt to debunk the sentiment-fraught season of Christmas by introducing a crass utilitarian note never quite comes off here.

And this same lack of gracefulness can be detected in "Reginald on the Academy" and "Reginald at the Theatre," wherein our sardonic imp of discord (he's only twenty-two) inveighs against the academy and the nomenclature of art as well as against the arbitrary laws of human conduct in society.

> "One goes to the Academy in self-defense," says Reginald. "It is the one topic one has in common with the country cousins." [1]

And further on:

> "The chief vice of the Academy," he continued, "is its nomenclature. Why, for instance, should an obvious trout-stream with a palpable rabbit sitting in the foreground be called an evening dream of unbeclouded peace, or something of that sort?" [2]

A sedate duchess who has the temerity to cross verbal foils with Reginald finds him equally outspoken in matters pertaining to religion and imperialism.

> "The Fashion just now is a Roman Catholic frame of mind with an Agnostic conscience: you get the mediaeval picturesqueness of the one with the modern conveniences of the other." [3]
> "Of course I accept the Imperial idea and the responsibility. After all, I would just as soon think in Continents as anywhere else. And some day, when the season is over, and we have the time, you shall explain to me the exact blood-brotherhood and

---

[1] Christopher Morley, ed., *The Short Stories of Saki* (London, 1949), p. 20. Hereafter *S. S.*

[2] *Ibid.*, p. 22.

[3] *Ibid.*, p. 23.

all that sort of thing that exists between a French Canadian and a mild Hindoo and a Yorkshireman, for instance."[4]

Passing over "Reginald's Peace Poem," which is pitched in the vein of low comedy and is nastily adolescent in taking to task poetasters, we come to one of the gems in the selection, "Reginald's Choir Treat." In this narrative Reginald engineers a miniature *chef-d'oeuvre.* He stage-manages a Sunday-school treat by depriving the choir boys of their clothes and compelling them to form a bacchanalian procession through the village with a he-goat and tin whistles, but no covering beyond a few polka-dotted handkerchiefs in the best style of our contemporary Bikini bathing suits:

> Reginald recognized the impossibility, in the time at his disposal, of teaching his shivering neophytes a chant in honour of Bacchus, so he started them off with a more familiar, if less appropriate, temperance hymn. After all, he said, it is the spirit of the thing that counts.[5]

Sad to relate, there were those benighted souls who did not wax enthusiastic over Reginald's escapade:

> Reginald's family never forgave him. They had no sense of humour.[6]

In the next six short stories plot interest is at a minimum and we are regaled by the nimble wit of Reginald as he deftly impales one foible of Society after another upon the relentless steel of the satirist's rapier. Not even Pope at his most splenetic is more scathing. Rare indeed are those few hardy ones who are not rendered *hors de combat* even after a superficial skirmish with Saki's protagonist. Aunts were always regarded by Reginald as fit grist for his malicious mill:

> "There's Marion Mulciber, who *would* think she could play

---

[4] *Ibid.,* p. 24.
[5] *Ibid.,* p. 29.
[6] *Ibid.,* p. 29.

bridge, just as she would think she could ride down a hill on a bicycle; on that occasion she went to a hospital; now she's gone into a Sisterhood—lost all she had, you know, and gave the rest to Heaven. Still, you can't call it a sudden calamity; *that* occurred when poor dear Marion was born. The doctors said at the time that she couldn't live more than a fortnight, and she's been trying ever since to see if she could. Women are *so* opinionated." [7]

Nor was he more tolerant of the affectations and ostentation of the *nouveaux riches,* so ludicrous in their excruciating endeavors to make the grade:

"I said to Lady Beauwhistle, if you want a lesson in elaborate artificiality, just watch the studied unconcern of a Persian cat entering a crowded salon, and then go and practise it for a fortnight. The Beauwhistles weren't born in the Purple, you know, but they're getting there on the instalment system—so much down, and the rest when you feel like it. They have kind hearts, and they never forget birthdays. I forget what he was, something in the city, where the patriotism comes from; and she—oh, well, her frocks are built in Paris, but she wears them with a strong English accent. So public-spirited of her. I think she must have been very strictly brought up, she's so desperately anxious to do the wrong thing correctly. Not that it really matters nowadays, as I told her. I know some perfectly virtuous people who are received everywhere." [8]

What it is significant to note here, aside from Saki's neat sting-in-the-tail technique, is something that becomes increasingly apparent the more one reads of this British writer's works. One cannot help but be aware that Saki's allegiance is to the prewar aristocratic tradition, which he admired even when he mocked. To be poor, humble, mediocre, was evidently a minor crime in his eyes, and plainly he himself may be accused of being a snob, albeit an engaging one. Unfortunately the enthralling humanity of Byron or Dickens is conspicuous by its absence in his work. At the same time, nevertheless, he was too intelligent

[7] *Ibid.,* p. 31.
[8] *Ibid.,* pp. 31–32.

and too cynical not to perceive the seamy side of the aristocratic "virtues." Hence it is that, like Swift, whose *saeva indignatio* lashed him into a fury over the turpitudes of the London Society he delighted to cut a figure in, Saki flays the social set whose child he was. One has little difficulty in, and ample justification for, visualizing Munro as very like his own Reginald in his youth, sardonic and rude at garden parties, never losing an opportunity to discomfit the sanctimony of a Pharisee, conversationally brilliant à la Wilde, as in

> "Scandal is merely the compassionate allowance which the gay make to the humdrum. Think how many blameless lives are brightened by the blazing indiscretions of other people."[9]

or in

> ". . . Isn't there a bishop or somebody who believes we shall meet all the animals we have known on earth in another world? How frightfully embarrassing to meet a whole shoal of whitebait you had last known at Prince's."[10]

But Wilde could never have hit on the refined irreverence of the following:

> "There may have been disillusionments in the lives of the mediaeval saints, but they would scarcely have been better pleased if they could have foreseen that their names would be associated nowadays chiefly with racehorses and the cheaper clarets."[11]

The vagaries and caprices of the female have always served as inviting targets for the satirist's ridicule, and although Reginald is by no means a misogynist, he seldom disappoints the male reader's expectations. Though he eschews the physical nausea of Swift and the tragic revulsion of Hamlet, he is not above the ridicule of the Meredithian comic spirit or the intellectual humor of the Shavian wit. Reginald is well aware that

---

9 *Ibid.*, p. 36.
10 *Ibid.*, p. 35.
11 *Ibid.*, pp. 37–38.

women and elephants never forget an injury.[12] And he never
seems to tire of relating old Lady Whortleberry's susceptibility
to screaming fits:

> "She's always been nervous since she lost her first husband.
> He died quite abruptly while watching a county cricket match;
> two and a half inches of rain had fallen for seven runs, and it was
> supposed that the excitement killed him. Anyhow, it gave her quite
> a shock; it was the first husband she's lost, you know, and now
> she always screams if anything thrilling happens too soon after
> dinner."[13]

A pixilated female's antics upon having overgorged herself
with really liqueur chocolates, with very little chocolate, provide
Reginald with one of his most hilarious anecdotal tidbits:

> "When the liqueurs began to take effect, she started to give
> them imitations of farmyard animals as they know them in Ber-
> mondsey. She began with a dancing bear, and you know Agatha
> doesn't approve of dancing, except at Buckingham Palace under
> proper supervision. And then she got up on the piano and gave
> them an organ monkey; I gather she went in for realism rather
> than a Maeterlinckian treatment of the subject. Finally she fell into
> the piano and said she was a parrot in a cage, and for an im-
> promptu performance I believe she was very word-perfect; no one
> had heard anything like it, except Baroness Boobelstein who has
> attended sittings of the Austrian Reichsrath. Agatha is trying the
> rest-cure at Buston."[14]

But it is in describing Mrs. Nicorax that Reginald really attains epic heights and even invites comparison with Fielding.
The episode which incited Mrs. Nicorax to charge him with in-
delicacy seems to come straight out of *Tom Jones* and, although
rather lengthy, well deserves a faithful transcription *in toto*:

---

[12] *Ibid.*, p. 40.
[13] *Ibid.*, p. 41.
[14] *Ibid.*, pp. 41–42.

"She went out riding with me, which was entirely her own suggestion, and as we were coming home through some meadows she made a quite unnecessary attempt to see if her pony would jump a rather messy sort of brook that was there. It wouldn't. It went with her as far as the water's edge, and from that point Mrs. Nicorax went on alone. Of course, I had to fish her out from the bank, and my riding-breeches are not cut with a view to salmon-fishing—it's rather an art even to ride in them. Her habit skirt was one of those open questions that need not be adhered to in emergencies, and on this occasion it remained behind in some water-weeds. She wanted me to fish about for that too, but I felt I had done enough Pharaoh's daughter business for an October afternoon, and I was beginning to want my tea. So I bundled her up to her pony and gave her a lead towards home as fast as I cared to go. What with the wet and the unusual responsibility, her abridged costume did not stand the pace, particularly well, and she got quite querulous when I shouted back that I had no pins with me—and no string. Some women expect so much from a fellow. When we got into the drive she wanted to go up the back way to the stables, but the ponies *know* they always get sugar at the front door, and I never attempt to hold a pulling pony; as for Mrs. Nicorax it took her all she knew to keep a firm hand on her seceding garments, which, as her maid remarked afterwards, were more *tout* than ensemble. Of course nearly the whole house-party were out on the lawn watching the sunset—the only day this month that it's occurred to the sun to show itself, as Mrs. Nic viciously observed—and I shall never forget the expression on her husband's face as we pulled up. 'My darling, this is too much!' was his first spoken comment; taking into consideration the state of her toilet, it was the most brilliant thing I had ever heard him say, and I went into the library to be alone and scream. Mrs. Nicorax says I have no delicacy." [15]

One could, of course, go on indefinitely detailing similar escapades just as Reginald does. It will, perhaps, be sufficient for our purpose, however, to rehearse just one more of Reginald's pranks, which occurs in "Reginald's Christmas Revel." It seems that Reginald was forced to spend Christmas at an in-

---

[15] *Ibid.,* pp. 43–44.

tolerably dull house, planning some diversion (a favorite plot trick of Munro). The entertainment he concocted on this occasion for the edification of all was by no means unworthy of his genius. But we shall let him tell it:

> "I had been preceded [to bed] a few minutes earlier by Miss Langshan-Smith, a rather formidable lady, who always got up at some uncomfortable hour in the morning, and gave you the impression that she had been in communication with most of the European governments before breakfast. There was a paper pinned on her door with a signed request that she might be recalled particularly early on the morrow. Such an opportunity does not come twice in a lifetime. I covered up everything except the signature with another notice, to the effect that before these words should meet the eye she would have ended a misspent life, was sorry for the trouble she was giving, and would like a military funeral. A few minutes later I violently exploded an air-filled paper bag on the landing, and gave a stage moan that could have been heard in the cellars. The noise these people made in forcing open the good lady's door was positively indecorous; she resisted gallantly, but I believe they searched her for bullets for about a quarter of an hour, as if she had been a historic battlefield."[16]

Comment here, no doubt, would be superfluous. Few will gainsay me if I submit that this is irresistibly funny. What is more, it is in Munro's most characteristic vein; he excels at this practical-joke sort of fun. Yet the significant fact, which is often lost sight of by those intent on accusing Saki of wanton cruelty, is that more often than not the laugh is incidental and the thought is fundamental. Therein lies the clue to the phenomenon of Hector Hugh Munro. There is an acrid quality to his mirth; it stings, but it does not heal. He is not so much in the tradition of Meredith and the Comic Spirit or Rabelais and the scatological quip as in the effete, sardonic vein of Wilde or the misanthropic ennui of Byron at his most bitter. In short, he is as essentially a satirist as a humorist. He is a British Lucian to whom the British

---

[16] *Ibid.*

Empire appeared as the Roman Empire appeared to Seneca as he watched Nero fire Rome.

THE "REGINALD IN RUSSIA" STORIES

Reginald in Russia (1910), Munro's second collection of short stories, is by no means equal in merit to his first one. It suffers, just as most sequels do, by seeking to exploit a vein that has already been mined dry. Although purportedly a further chronicle of Reginald's doings, the reader finds Reginald appearing in only the first of the fifteen stories. Consequently, one not only misses his inimitable urbane malice and humor, but is frequently surprised into a mood of pleasurable expectation in anticipation of the superior laugh only to be brought up rudely and abruptly by a macabre type of humor not very far removed from the kind to be found in Faulkner's *As I Lay Dying*. To put it in another way, we can say that Munro in this second collection is much more in earnest in castigating the failings of his society. By the same token, however, his satire is less effective.

For true satire demands a certain objectivity though not an absolute one. The effective satirist must be neither too biased nor too angry. If he is the former, his work degenerates into vituperation. One of the great weaknesses of satire since World War I is that it is far too propagandistic. Saki, to be sure, cannot be arraigned on the charge of propaganda. Social consciousness he does possess, but it is not of the militaristic kind. His humor, which brings insight and tolerance, is his saving grace. And yet one finds it difficult not to suspect rancor and something deeper than good-natured animosity in Reginald's flippancy regarding the clergy:

> ". . . in the Anglican Church in a certain capital, which shall be nameless, I was present the other day when one of the junior chaplains was preaching in aid of distressed something or other,

and he brought a really eloquent passage to a close with the remark,
'The tears of the afflicted, to what shall I liken them—to diamonds?' The other junior chaplain, who had been dozing out of
professional jealousy, awoke with a start and asked hurriedly,
'Shall I play to diamonds, partner?' It didn't improve matters
when the senior chaplain remarked dreamily, but with painful
distinctness, 'Double diamonds.' Every one looked at the preacher,
half expecting him to redouble, but he contented himself with
scoring what points he could under the circumstances." [17]

Now it may be pointed out that Burns, Byron, and Shelley
attacked the so-called hypocrisy of the clergy in much less uncertain terms than these; that Blake's diatribes against institu-
tionalized religion partake much more of vituperation than
the comparatively innocuous jibe of Reginald.

Nevertheless, the poetic polemics of the aforementioned
four breathe a fervor and earnestness that elicit, if not a sympathetic, at least a patient hearing from the reader; whereas Saki
here is obviously being merely nasty and beneath the intelligent
reader's notice. One has the feeling that no real animus for reform informs Saki's satire here; that he is idly jesting merely for
the sake of jesting. One is indeed reminded of Bacon's "jesting
Pilate" and his disconcerting rhetorical question to Jesus. There
may perhaps be those who would insist on defending Saki's
Reginald here by recalling to us that the main object of satire
is to point out the discrepancy between what a person or object
may pretend to be and what it really is, so that the truth will
emerge for all to profit by it. We cannot agree.

"The Reticence of Lady Anne," the second short story, gives
us our first glimpse into the Saki who could jest over death. It
is a masterful short story and by far the best in the selection. The
impact of the last sentence on the reader is as devastating as the
last sentence in Faulkner's "A Rose for Emily." The gasp of
surprise one gives vent to as he finishes the story is, of course,

---

[17] *Ibid.*, p. 56.

a well-calculated effect on the part of the author and a common device, moreover, of the storyteller's art. But not even Hemingway ever wielded it as consummately as Saki does here. An excerpt can hardly do justice to Munro's art but must, notwithstanding, be given for the sake of completeness:

> Egbert came into the large, dimly lit drawing-room with the air of a man who is not certain whether he is entering a dovecote or a bomb factory . . . The little domestic quarrel over the luncheon-table had not been fought to a definite finish, and the question was how far Lady Anne was in a mood to renew or forgo [*sic*] hostilities. Her pose in the arm-chair by the tea-table was rather elaborately rigid . . . Egbert poured himself out some tea . . . "My remark at luncheon had a purely academic application," he announced, "you seem to put an unnecessarily personal significance into it."
>
> Lady Anne maintained her defensive barrier of silence.
>
> "Don't you think we're being rather foolish?" said Egbert cheerfully.
>
> If Lady Anne thought so she didn't say so . . .
>
> "I daresay the fault has been partly on my side," continued Egbert, with evaporating cheerfulness. "After all, I'm only human, you know. You seem to forget that I'm only human . . ."
>
> Lady Anne showed no sign of being impressed.
>
> Egbert looked at her nervously . . .
>
> "I shall go and dress for dinner," he announced in a voice into which he intended some shade of sternness to creep.
>
> At the door a final excess of weakness impelled him to make a further appeal.
>
> "Aren't we being very silly? . . ."
>
> Lady Anne made no sign . . . She had been dead for two hours.[18]

Here is comic irony at its best, and here the esthetic pleasure is not lessened by the fact that we detect some quality of the practical joke. Frankly, it is difficult to find anything to compare with it except possibly the opening scene of Henry Becque's play *La Parisienne*. One cannot help but feel that, had Munro

---

[18] *Ibid.*, pp. 58–61.

written more frequently in this vein and less frequently in the Reginald vein, he might have been a greater artist though a less efficacious critic of Society and society. Yet to those who recognize the large role irony plays in Munro's work, his view of life is more discouraging even than outspoken pessimism. It cannot be laughed aside like the gloom of an Ecclesiastes, because it laughs itself and forestalls the mockery of an unwilling hearer. "The Reticence of Lady Anne" is disconcerting if for no other reason than that it puts one in mind of Aldous Huxley's "of such is the Kingdom of Heaven." The real tragedy is not that of Lady Anne—no one will miss her—but that of Egbert and the thousands who like him are martyrs of marital law.

The third selection, "The Lost Sanjak," is a tedious and pointless rehearsal of the irony of events which condemn an innocent man to death. "The Sex That Doesn't Shop" endeavors to be clever in satirizing women shoppers but succeeds only in being facetious. "The Blood-Feud of Toad-Water" has recourse to *reductio ad absurdum* in ridiculing the mighty causes that often arise from trivial things. Unfortunately for Saki, however, he here essays a subject which Samuel Langhorne Clemens had treated so masterfully in *Huckleberry Finn*. As a result, he suffers by comparison, for Mrs. Saunders and Mrs. Grick cannot even hope to stand up to the Grangefords and Shepherdsons. "A Young Turkish Catastrophe" is too trivial and inane to merit comment. And the same applies to "Judkin of the Parcels." "Gabriel-Ernest" is worthy of comment only because it is the first of Munro's stories that deal with werewolves. How to account for this morbid fascination with lycanthropy on our author's part is another question which, perhaps, is best left to the psychologists. It may be that Munro, like Pascal and Swift, desired to call attention to the beast in man. Simonides, it will be recalled, saw women as foxes, bitches, polecats, and mares. Then again, Munro may be simply satirizing the multitude who cling blindly to their prejudices. It is even conceivable that as a child he was subject to nightmares. It is a well-recognized fact that comic absurdity is of the same nature as that of dreams. But no doubt the real explanation lies in Bergson's definition of a humorist as "a moralist disguised as a scientist, something like an anatomist who practises dissection with the sole object of filling us with disgust . . ."[19]

"The Saint and the Goblin" is a flippant treatment of religious hypocrisy somewhat in the vein of Shaw's *Major Barbara*. "The Soul of Laploshka" is an admirable study in avarice with a suggestion of the supernatural thrown in for good measure. On a small scale, one can even venture to say that it is not unworthy of Molière or Balzac. The portrait of Laploshka, who indulged "in agonies of perjury rather than admit the incriminating possession of a copper coin when change was needed to tip a waiter,"[20] is indeed a gem of caricature. "The Bag" narrates the confusion that arises when a polecat is mistaken for a fox. It is one of the altogether too frequent times when Saki nods, and with Queen Victoria we are tempted to say, "We are not amused." When Saki is good, he is really superb; when he fails, he is, alas, lugubrious. "The Strategist" is another take-off on the insufferable boredom and frivolity of house parties. The title refers to Rollo, who is a less-interesting Reginald but has the latter's propensity for playing practical jokes on tedious hosts. "Cross Currents" utilizes the eternal triangle for its plot interest and gives us three memorable portraits in the best of the Saki tradition. The woman is Vanessa, who discovers "that a husband who added a roving disposition to a settled income was a mixed blessing."[21] Becoming bored with her husband Clyde, who is given to leisurely peregrinations in esoteric lands, she takes up with a certain Dobrinton, whom she first met in a Caucasian town. The friendship blossoms into love, and

19 Henri Bergson, *Laughter* (New York, 1911), p. 128.
20 *S. S.,* pp. 88–89.
21 *Ibid.,* p. 105.

it is not long before Clyde is reading a long letter from Vanessa
"justifying her action in flitting to more civilized lands with a
more congenial companion."[22] But as luck would have it, Vanessa and her third inamorato—she was a widow when she married
Clyde—are captured by Kurdish brigands. And soon after her
husband turns up as a captive too:

> And so, in the cramped quarters of a mountain hut, the ill-
> assorted trio watched the insufferable hours crawl slowly by.
> Dobrinton was too frightened to be conversational; Vanessa was
> too mortified to open her lips; and Clyde was moodily silent.[23]

One evening, "finding that he was not getting the attention
to which he was entitled,"[24] Clyde escapes. A few days later, the
other two are duly ransomed and released. But the Furies pur-
sue Dobrinton with hateful malice:

> . . . Dobrinton was bitten by a dog which was assumed to be mad,
> though it may only have been indiscriminating. The victim did not
> wait for symptoms of rabies to declare themselves, but died forth-
> with of fright . . . [25]

Poor Vanessa, in time divorced by Clyde, ended up on the kitch-
en staff of a West End Club. The moral is a trite one—as jejune
as Flaubert's *Bovary*—but this is one time when Saki scores with
telling effect, neatly deflating the romance of adultery and
ridiculing the plight of social climbers like Vanessa.

"The Baker's Dozen" is written in the form of a dialogue
between an elderly gentleman and a middle-aged woman—both
widowed—who meet on the deck of a steamship. Their court-
ship threatens to terminate when it is discovered they have
thirteen children between them. However, everything turns out
right in the end when it is discovered that they had miscounted
and there were only twelve:

[22] *Ibid.*, p. 106.
[23] *Ibid.*, p. 107.
[24] *Ibid.*, p. 108.
[25] *Ibid.*

EMILY: Richard!
RICHARD: Emily! *(They embrace.)*[26]

The concluding tale of the collection, "The Mouse," is written somewhat in the same vein as "The Reticence of Lady Anne." The grotesque humor here arises from the fact that a male passenger sitting in a train compartment with a lady suddenly discovers a mouse has crawled up his leg. Since the lady is asleep at the time, he audaciously ventures to remove his trousers and rid himself of the mouse. His efforts are crowned with success, but before he has put his trousers on again, the lady's awakening embarrasses him. It is only at the end that he discovers she is blind.

Although, as we stated at the outset, this second collection of Saki's short stories is not of high merit, it is important to the student in that it reveals to us the peculiar nature of the author's humor, which is actually the counterpart to his irony. Sometimes the writer states what ought to be done, and pretends to believe that this is just what is actually being done; then we have irony. Sometimes, on the other hand, the writer describes with scrupulous minuteness what is being done, and pretends to believe that this is just what ought to be done; such is often the method of humor. Both are forms of satire, however. And that is what one must never lose sight of in reading Saki. It is the reason why his short stories often require repeated readings to be comprehended fully.

"THE CHRONICLES OF CLOVIS"

THE third collection of H. H. Munro's stories—twenty-eight in all—contains by far the best work that he did in this genre. In it we find the tales that are the most frequently anthologized by

---

[26] *Ibid.*, p. 114.

editors of the short story. And in Clovis we find a worthy successor to the incomparable Reginald. Clovis Sangrail, in fact, is an exquisite projection of adolescent ambition and, in boyhood brutality, frequently surpasses his worthy predecessor.

The Chronicles of Clovis (1911) reveal Saki at his most characteristic. Nowhere else does his work evince the extraordinary play of mind that we find here. Nowhere else does he display such force, such mastery over his medium. Here, indeed, we find Saki's plenty: his understanding of, and love for, animals—frequently in preference to human beings—his almost inhuman aloofness from suffering, his firsthand knowledge of house parties and hunting, his uncanny felicity in satirical nomenclature, his gift for epigram and mordant irony, his penchant for practical jokes, his power of evoking an atmosphere of pure horror, his Dickensian appreciation of food and the importance of its place in life, his adeptness in making capital plot use of eerie, rustic superstitions, and his inexhaustible repertory of bizarre and startling plots.

But it is here, also, that we discover Saki at his least amiable and his most Swiftian. His prose possesses a chilling, ironic detachment, and seems always to owe its convincing justness to, at his least actively malicious, a coldly intense scrutiny, a potentially hostile attention. Saki's dispassionate, matter-of-fact tone induces a feeling and a motion of assent, a trust in the solid ground, before he suddenly opens the pitfalls and the reader finds himself helplessly falling down. We often feel the effect of the words as an intensity in the castigator rather than as an effect upon a victim. And this we cannot help thinking is conditioned by some frustration and constriction on the author's part. The point may be enforced by comparing Saki's irony with Gibbon's irony in the fifteenth chapter of *The Rise and Fall of the Roman Empire.* Gibbon's irony habituates and reassures, ministering to a kind of judicial certitude or complacency. Saki's

irony, like Swift's, is essentially a matter of surprise and negation; its function is to defeat habit, to intimidate, and to de-
moralize. But Swift often redeems himself by an emotional intensity, little trace of which is to be found in Saki.

Like Pope, Saki seems to have been fascinated by the effects
that at the same time seem to evoke a more exciting reality than
that of common sense. And in creating these effects he is un-
doubtedly registering certain insistent qualities of experience as
it came to him, Victorian though he was. Like O. Henry, moreover, Saki had a genius for odd circumstance, the surprising
incident, and the liveliest of eyes for human frailties and the
jibes of Dame Fortune. His delight is to trick expectation and
confound accepted ideas. He makes games of *Homo sapiens*
who presumptuously claims to be an *animal rationale,* and the
effect is often painful if not outright sadistic. In fact, the tempta-
tion to explain Saki by recourse to pathology is an inviting one,
except that comedy and introversion are contradictory terms. It
is perhaps safer and sounder to explain him by his milieu—the
cosmic despair of the late nineteenth and early twentieth cen-
turies, which left a spiritual vacuum in the place of traditional
religion. In this way, it can be understood why Saki's humor and
irony frequently strike one as self-conceit and self-indulgence
rather than self-realization. In this presumptuousness we readily
discern a Swiftian egoism, and, behind this latter, something less
spontaneous and more bitter, the beginnings, in fact, of a
curious ennui that becomes more pronounced as the laughter
more closely analyzes his laughter.

"Esme," the initial tale of this third collection, is, under its
surface equanimity, a savage indictment of the depravity of
human nature. A Baroness is telling a hunting story to Clovis.
She describes how she was riding one day with an acquaintance,
Constance Broddle, and how they encountered an escaped
hyaena, which she christened Esme on the spot. This callous

indifference with which the Baroness watches Esme devour a lost gypsy infant could only have been etched by Saki:

> Constance shuddered. "Do you think the poor little thing suffered much? . . ."
> "The indications were all that way," I said; "on the other hand, of course, it may have been crying from sheer temper. Children sometimes do." [27]

But the crowning touch to this Borgian comedy is yet to come. When the hounds of a young nobleman devour Esme in turn, the Baroness has the brazen gall to demand reparation for the death of what she claims was her favorite dog:

> "You have killed my Esme," I exclaimed bitterly. . . .
> "He took second in the puppy class at Birmingham last year," I said resolutely.
> Constance snorted loudly.
> "Don't cry, dear," I said brokenly; "it was all over in a moment. He couldn't have suffered much."
> "Look here," said the young fellow desperately, "you simply must let me do something by way of reparation."
> I refused sweetly, but as he persisted I let him have my address. [27]

At this point in the narrative, the Baroness pauses reflectively, whether for dramatic effect or simply to savor her own refined cruelty, Saki does not vouchsafe to say. But the smirk of depraved satisfaction can be seen even though it is not described as convulsing her harsh physiognomy. Then she continues sweetly:

> There was a sequel to the adventure, though. I got through the post a charming little diamond brooch, with the name Esme set in a sprig of rosemary. Incidentally, too, I lost the friendship of Constance Broodle. You see, when I sold the brooch I quite properly refused to give her any share of the proceeds. I pointed out that the

------

[27] *S. S.,* pp. 122–23.

Esme part of the affair was my own invention, and the hyaena part of it belonged to Lord Pabham; if it really was his hyaena, of which, of course, I've no proof.[28]

And yet there are those who feel the melancholy Dane's vituperation on womankind was too biased, that a misogynist is abnormal and that Munro should have married!

By-passing "The Match-Maker," which is of no moment, we come to "Tobermory," the story of a cat that suddenly stampeded a house party as the result of its acquired ability to converse in human fashion and to deliver itself of precise extracts from the private opinions of each of those present about the other:

> "What do you think of human intelligence?" asked Mavis Pellington lamely.
>
> "Of whose intelligence in particular?" asked Tobermory coldly.
>
> "Oh, well, mine for instance," said Mavis, with a feeble laugh.
>
> "You put me in an embarrassing position," said Tobermory, whose tone and attitude certainly did not suggest a shred of embarrassment. "When your inclusion in this house-party was suggested Sir Wilfrid protested that you were the most brainless woman of his acquaintance, and that there was a wide distinction between hospitality and the care of the feeble-minded. Lady Stanley replied that your lack of brain-power was the precise quality which had earned you your invitation, as you were the only person she could think of who might be idiotic enough to buy their old car. You know, the one they call 'The Envy of Sisyphus,' because it goes quite nicely up-hill if you push it." [29]

It is quite understandable why, after a few more sallies of this sort, everyone agrees that Tobermory "must go." They are saved the trouble of poisoning him, however, by Tobermory himself, who goes the way of all feline flesh by falling in combat with

---

28 *Ibid.*, pp. 123–24.
29 *Ibid.*, pp. 129–30.

the big Tom from the Rectory, who evidently did not recognize Tobermory's priority claims on a tortoise-shell puss. And Mr. Appin, alas, met an equally mute and inglorious demise:

> Tobermory had been Appin's one successful pupil, and he was destined to have no successor. A few weeks later an elephant in the Dresden Zoological Garden, which had shown no previous signs of irritability, broke loose and killed an Englishman who had apparently been teasing it. The victim's name was variously reported in the papers as Oppin and Eppelin, but his front name was faithfully rendered Cornelius.
>
> "If he was trying German irregular verbs on the poor beast," said Clovis, "he deserved all he got."[30]

"Mrs. Packletide's Tiger," the next tale, is another edifying study of the vanity and avariciousness of womankind somewhat in the manner of "Esme." Mrs. Packletide's consuming passion in life is to shoot a live tiger. The co-operative natives of India oblige her by luring a senile specimen of the species within rifle range. Unfortunately, however, some rather disconcerting complications arise. Mrs. Packletide, to be sure, does not fall victim to amateur hunter's fright—her own hide is too tough for that. She sights and shoots, and the striped beast of prey very considerately drops dead. But a post mortem, at which Mrs. Packletide's companion-in-hunting, Louisa Mebbin, is present, reveals the startling fact that the tiger died of heart failure, and that Mrs. Packletide's bullet had missed him and killed, instead, a goat that had been used as "bait-lure." Our Victorian Diana, of course, is not denied her social triumph, but Miss Mebbin sees to it that she is adequately reimbursed for maintaining a discreet silence about the whole affair.

"The Stampeding of Lady Bastable" regales us with one of the Katzenjammer-like pranks of Clovis. The mother of this adorable *enfant terrible,* after a great amount of cajolery, manages to persuade Lady Bastable to keep Clovis in her house for

---

[30] *Ibid.,* p. 134.

six days by agreeing to cancel Lady Bastable's outstanding bridge account. These arrangements, however, do not seem to meet with the unqualified approval of the principal personage involved. Clovis, knowing the lady's weak spot (her dread of revolution) sees a means to remedy his predicament. So on the particular morning of this story, he rushes into the servants' quarters and shouts:

> "Poor Lady Bastable! In the morning-room! Oh, quick!"[31]

Then he rushes madly through her room, where she was seated quietly reading the paper, and shrieks at her in passing, "The jacquerie! They're on us!"[32]

Not even the "mad" Hamlet pursued by Rosencrantz and Guildenstern through the labyrinthine passageways of the Danish palace ever created such pandemonium incarnate:

> The scared mob of servants burst in on his heels, the gardener still clutching the sickle with which he had been trimming hedges, and the impetus of their headlong haste carried them, slipping and sliding, over the smooth, parquet flooring towards the chair where their mistress sat in panic-stricken amazement. If she had had a moment granted her for reflection she would have behaved, as she afterwards explained, with considerable dignity. It was probably the sickle which decided her, but anyway she followed the lead that Clovis had given her through the French window, and ran well and far across the lawn before the eyes of her astonished retainers.[33]

Needless to say, after this refreshing diversion, Lady Bastable was only too glad to pay her bridge debt to Mrs. Sangrail for the privilege of *not* having Clovis as a week-long guest.

"The Background" is of no consequence whatever, and the formidable-sounding "Herman the Irascible—A Story of the Great Weep" is nothing but a rather flat *reductio ad absurdum*

---

[31] *Ibid.,* p. 141.
[32] *Ibid.*
[33] *Ibid.*

on woman suffrage. "The Unrest-Cure" is considerably more
lively than these and again brings Clovis to the forefront as a
practical joker. In this instance our peerless youth-without-
benefit-of-the-Grace-of-the-Grail manages to panic a staid, middle-aged bachelor and his old-maidenish sister by a "fake" mas-
sacre of the Jews in their neighborhood.

"The Jesting of Arlington Stringham" is merely a prelude
to what is perhaps the outstanding story in the volume, namely,
"Sredni Vashtar." The first of the two tells of a domestic tragedy in which the wife of a prominent politician discovers his
infidelity by being told that the sparkling display of witty humor
her husband suddenly finds himself possessed of on the floor of
the House derives from a certain Lady Isobel. Saki's quiet close
to the narrative is like the final twist of the screw on the torture
rack, which sends the victim from agonizing pain into welcome
oblivion:

> "So that is where he gets his humour," said Eleanor slowly,
> and the hard lines deepened round her mouth.
> The death of Eleanor Stringham from an overdose of chloral,
> occurring at the end of a rather uneventful session, excited a cer-
> tain amount of unobtrusive speculation. Clovis, who perhaps ex-
> aggerated the importance of curry in the home, hinted at domestic
> sorrow.
> And, of course, Arlington never knew. It was the tragedy
> of his life that he should miss the fullest effect of his jesting.[34]

But for those who delight in the gruesome there is the incomparable "Sredni Vashtar," which loses nothing by comparison with the Gothic novel. And as for irony of character
(in which a person's true character is shown to be in painfully
comic contrast to his appearance or manner), it would not be
misguided zeal for Saki to compare it with *Death of a Salesman*.
The story tells of a delicate, small boy, ten-year-old Conradin,
who lived under the strictest surveillance of a religious aunt,

---

[34] *Ibid.*, p. 158.

Mrs. de Ropp. Thwarting him for his own good was a duty that Mrs. de Ropp found very pleasurable. Conradin hid in the tool-shed a Houdan hen of which he was very fond. But his tyrannical overseer discovered and sold it. Then, from a butcher boy, Conradin got a big polecat-ferret and hid it in the same place. Then, every night, he prayed to it as to a god. Every evening Conradin's bitter litany went up: "Do one thing for me, Sredni Vashtar." Mrs. de Ropp, noticing his visits to the shed, got the key and went in to make a personal investigation, while Conradin, his face glued to the dining-room window, prayed for vengeance. She did not come out. But after what to Conradin seemed an interminable interval, he saw a long, low, yellow-and-brown beast emerge with dark, wet stains around the fur of his throat and jaws. After a while the maids go to hunt for their mistress while Conradin calmly makes tea, with much butter on his toast. Suddenly he hears shrieks and scared sobbings. "Whoever will break it to the poor child? I couldn't for the life of me." And while they debate among themselves, Conradin makes himself more toast . . .[35]

After the tense and strained atmosphere of "Sredni Vashtar," it is a welcome relief to return again to the antics of Clovis in "Adrian," which is very similar to "Reginald's Christmas Revel." In this instance Clovis contents himself with being a passive onlooker, while Adrian of Bethnal Green amuses himself by transferring the bathroom label in a German hotel to the adjoining bedroom door belonging to Frau Hofrath Schilling, who, from seven o'clock in the morning onward, had a stream of involuntary visitors.

"The Chaplet" returns us to the purer regions of irony again

---

[35] The event in this story is so startling and horrible that it is likely to overshadow the irony of character and to suggest, at first glance, irony of events. But the event in itself is not ironical; the ironic "twist" of the ending is the grotesque contrast between the truth and the appearance of the child murderer. "Whoever will break it to the poor child?" We can see the smirk on the "poor child's" lips. If they only knew!

with some slapstick thrown in for good measure. It tells of a
chef of a famous restaurant, Monsieur Aristide Sancourt, who
plunges the head of an orchestra leader into the boiling contents of a soup tureen because the guests had allowed his "chef-
d'œuvre, Canetons à la mode d'Ambleve," to grow cold on their
plates while they listened to the strains of "The Chaplet."

> Whether the leader of the orchestra died from drowning by
> soup, or from the shock to his professional vanity, or was scalded
> to death, the doctors were never wholly able to agree. Monsieur
> Aristide Sancourt, who now lives in complete retirement, always
> inclined to the drowning theory.[36]

"The Quest" and "Wratislov" represent another barren
and arid spot in the collection. The former is simply built
around a case of mistaken identity while the latter contains
one of the most gauche puns in literature: "Conscience makes
cowboys of us all." [37]

"The Easter Egg" is an unusual story because for once Saki
seems to be in deadly earnest, and narrates for us a straight-
forward and tragic tale with not the least trace of irony. It
tells of the heroic sacrifice a mother makes to save her cowardly
son from certain death. Saki's intent here, we frankly admit, is
a puzzle to us. He seldom contents himself with a plain narrative lacking completely in twists of any kind.

"Filboid Studge" is Saki's take-off on advertising, and here
we find ourselves on the familiar soil of satire. This is the story
of a penurious young man who wanted to marry the daughter
of a patent-food seller. Mark Spayley, the prospective bride-
groom, steps in to save his future father-in-law from ruin.
As Pipenta the food had failed to sell; Spayley rechristened it
Filboid Studge, and designed one huge, somber poster depict-
ing the damned in hell suffering a new torment from their in-
ability to get at Filboid Studge, which elegant young fiends

---

[36] *S. S.*, p. 171.
[37] *Ibid.*, p. 180.

held out just beyond their reach. The scene was rendered more gruesome by a subtle suggestion of the features of the leading men and women of the day. The poster bore no fulsome allusions to the merits of the new breakfast food, but a single grim statement: "They cannot buy it now."

Spayley had grasped the fact that people will do things from a sense of duty that they would never contemplate as a pleasure. Unfortunately, however, he did not perceive that this elementary bolus of psychology had a bearing on his own personal problems. Needless to say, he lost his bride-to-be as a result of the phenomenal success of his poster. Her father, it seems, now that she was an heiress, decided she should have something better than a two-hundred-a-year poster designer. Any individual human want may be satisfied, but the sum total of human wants is insatiable. However, Clovis, not being Veblen, could only console Mark by pointing out that it is not for mortals to countermand success.

"The Music on the Hill" is a rather eerie tale with its share of grotesque irony. It is extremely atmospheric in the Brontë and Hardy tradition, while its horrific effects put one in mind of Doyle and Collins. S. P. B. Mais takes this story quite seriously. He writes:

> From "The Music on the Hill" we learn that "Saki" held in very considerable awe the power of the great god Pan: his lonely life as a boy in North Devon must have led him to realise that the forces of Nature are relentless and terrible. This fact must have been seared into his heart, for he recurs to it again and again. The doing to death of the young city-bred wife by the hunted stag because of her disbelief in the power of the wood-gods is horribly effective in its irony.[38]

Frankly, we are inclined to be skeptical. We do not deny Munro's predilection for the ghoulish and sadistic. But when we are asked to swallow Munro's awe for Pan, we must beg

---

[38] S. P. B. Mais, *Books and Their Writers* (New York, 1920), p. 321.

to demur. We suspect that in this isolated instance even the
keen-sighted Mr. Mais has allowed himself to be hoodwinked
by our master ironist, unless, of course, the critic himself is
being ironical. At any rate, we must urge the caution that
although Pan is indispensable to the understanding of D. H.
Lawrence and Wallace Stevens, he is not at all germane to
the comprehension of Saki. Nevertheless, there is no denying
that even a Joseph Conrad or a Robert Louis Stevenson would
have been envious of such an ending as—

> "Drive it off!" she shrieked. But the figure made no answering.
> The antlers drove straight at her breast, the acrid smell of the
> hunted animal was in her nostrils, but her eyes were filled with the
> terror of somthing she saw other than her oncoming death. And
> in her ears rang the echo of a boy's laughter, golden and
> equivocal.[39]

That could even have come straight out of Paul Bowles, Truman
Capote, or Norman Mailer.

"The Story of St. Vespaluus" is a delectable satire on religion spiced with the horrors of Roman barbarism. The name
Vespaluus itself is a composite of Paul, the Christian saint,
and Vespasian, the Roman tyrant, under whose reign Jerusalem
was destroyed and the Jews persecuted. It admirably sums up
the character of the "hero" in Munro's tale. Vespaluus is the
favorite nephew of the king, Hkrikros, and the heir to the
pagan throne. Being a recalcitrant child, however, he delights
in angering the king by professing Christian sympathies. When
a series of mildly primitive measures fail to convince Vespaluus
of the error of his ways, the king is roused to fury and orders
him to be stung to death by three hives of bees. Since, however,
the chief keeper of the bees, being secretly a pious Christian
himself, had remained at work all the previous night in disarming all, or almost all, of the hives' inmates, the king's carefully
planned entertainment ends in a fiasco:

---

[39] *S. S.,* p. 193.

. . . [Vespaluus] was wrapped from head to foot in bees; each individual insect nursed the dreadful and humiliating knowledge that in this supreme hour of catastrophe it could not sting, but each felt that it ought to pretend to. Vespaluus squealed and wriggled with laughter, for he was being tickled nearly to death . . .[40]

The apoplectic king, of course, soon dies of humiliation, and a frenzied and fanatical public rushes Vespaluus to the throne in religious ecstasy. Imagine, if you will, the chagrin of the newly crowned king's chamberlain when he discovers his monarch is still a confirmed pagan:

The Chamberlain wrung his hands despairingly.

"But, your Majesty," he wailed, "the people are reverencing you as a saint, and the nobles are being Christianized in batches, and neighboring potentates of that Faith are sending special envoys to welcome you as a brother . . . you can't surely go back on all this."

"I don't mind being reverenced and greeted and honored," said Vespaluus; "I don't even mind being sainted in moderation, as long as I'm not expected to be saintly as well. But I wish you clearly and finally to understand that I will *not* give up the worship of the august and auspicious serpents."[41]

A satisfactory compromise, however, was reached:

At stated intervals the king appeared before his subjects in the national cathedral in the character of St. Vespaluus, and the idolatrous grove was gradually pruned and lopped away until nothing remained of it. But the sacred and esteemed serpents were removed to a private shrubbery in the royal gardens, where Vespaluus the Pagan and certain members of his household devoutly and decently worshipped them.[42]

"The Way to the Dairy" is a wryly amusing sketch of the Brimley Bromefields, a group of nieces who suddenly become concerned at the loneliness of an aunt's life when, from being

---

[40] *Ibid.,* p. 198.
[41] *Ibid.,* p. 200.
[42] *Ibid.,* p. 201.

unobtrusively poor, she becomes quite pleasantly rich. Here we feel Munro had a subject that could justifiably have been treated in more somber tone. For avarice is one of the principal vices attacked by the confirmed satirist. Saki treats it as a foible. One need only recall Ben Jonson's *Volpone* and *The Alchemist* and Molière's *L'Avare* to appreciate the heights which the treatment of miserliness can attain. For one reason or another, however, Saki did not choose to be severely censorious in this tale. He contented himself with the mild irony of having the heiress aunt become a gambling addict with the too-obvious consequences.

"The Peace Offering" introduces us to Clovis the dramatist. Always ready to oblige in almost anything, Clovis agrees to aid his Baroness friend in staging an amateur theatrical. Inevitably, Clovis and the Baroness find themselves at variance in regard to certain lines contained in the Trojan tragedy they are preparing to perform. When the Baroness wantonly mutilates some choice verses of Clovis's own invention, that young man remains ostensibly unruffled, but like the narrator in Edgar Allan Poe's "The Cask of Amontillado," he vows revenge. He personally and assiduously coaches the young lady who is to impersonate Cassandra, and his conception of that mad prophetess, it seems, is at one with that of Robinson Jeffers'. The reader therefore is not at all surprised when, on the evening of the performance, at which many prominent political figures are gathered, Cassandra blurts out in her first speech:

> "I see woe for this fair country if the brood of corrupt, self-seeking, unscrupulous, unprincipled politicians" (here she named one of the two rival parties in the State) "continue to infest and poison our local councils and undermine our Parliamentary representation; if they continue to snatch votes by nefarious and discreditable means . . ."[43]

That was as far as she got. At this point her audience proved

---

[43] *Ibid.,* p. 213.

as skeptical of vatic utterance as their foolish forebears, and walked out. The Baroness was accused of outrageously bad taste and tactlessness. Clovis agreed.

"The Peace of Mowsle Barton" sets out to prove the oft-repeated comment that sometimes one can find the city much more restful than the country. This is the truth that Crefton Lockyer discovers when he seeks the quietude of the farm-yard at Mowsle Barton during his summer vacation. For a time he enjoys himself. But soon alarming distractions beset him. He finds himself in the midst of a witches' feud and con-stantly is assailed by the bickerings of Betsy Croot and Martha Pillamon, who are constantly raining spells on each other. Finally, after a series of untoward accidents (in one of which three floating ducks disappear completely under water) that had been threatened by one or the other of the two "hags," he hurriedly packs up his belongings and returns to the quiet of London.

"The Talking-Out of Tarrington" is pure persiflage, but "The Hounds of Fate" puts one very much in mind of Thomas Hardy both in plot and in setting. It represents one of the purest examples of the irony of events (dramatic irony) to be found in all of Saki. "The Recessional" is another hilarious parody of the aspirants to Parnassus, very much in the vein of "Reginald's Peace Poem." "A Matter of Sentiment" is a rather inspid piece on horse racing, while "The Secret Sin of Septimus Brope" is a masterful albeit conventional comedy of a prim cleric who supplements the meager income he derives from disseminating the Holy Gospel by writing lyrics for popular songs. "Ministers of Grace" utilizes the supernatural much in the comic vein that Noel Coward does in *Blithe Spirit*. The story is about a certain Duke of Scaw who is a master in "koepenickery," that is, the art of summoning angelic forces to assume the guise of living politicians while the latter are temporarily spirited away for safekeeping. The accord that he manages to effect in Parliament by his art is really amazing. The last selection, "The Remoulding of Groby Lington" could have been written only by Saki. It could be dismissed as utter nonsense, were it not for the fact that it reminds one of Eugene O'Neill's *The Hairy Ape*. For the main character of the tale, Groby Lington, is very much inclined to assume the mannerisms of whatever pet animal he happens to favor at any particular time. This fact is first brought home to him when he observes that a sketch of himself drawn by one of his nephews looks very much like his parrot. When his brother, Colonel John, brings him a monkey, Groby becomes fascinated by the animal, and it is not long before he begins playing genuine monkey-shines on his horrified friends, who, for some strange reason, come to regard him as insane. Unfortunately, the monkey dies prematurely.

"BEASTS AND SUPER-BEASTS," "THE TOYS OF PEACE" AND "THE SQUARE EGG"

ALTHOUGH Munro wrote novels (which we propose to discuss in the next chapter of this study), there can be little doubt that his claim to fame will ultimately be based on his artistry in the short story. For as we are trying to show, it was in this branch of letters that he was a past master. *Beasts and Super-Beasts* (1914), the worthy successor to *Clovis*, leaves little doubt in our minds on this point. Containing thirty-six tales in all, some of which excel even the most witty chapters of *The Chronicles of Clovis*, it represents another triumph for Munro in the humorously ironic ridicule of man's inhumanity to man, as well as in the exposé of the selfish, petty, and crassly material-istic motives that serve as the unedifying springs of human conduct. As may be surmised from the title, Munro concerns himself in this collection primarily with animal stories, and his practical jokes are engineered for the most part by the inventive genius of sixteen-year-old flappers instead of by those young male prodigals, sybarites, and mischief-makers, Reginald and Clovis.

The comment of S. P. B. Mais on Saki's inanely unusual choice of animals for this set of stories is extremely illuminating:

> . . . they bear something of the same resemblance to ordinary animals and ordinary names as Heath Robinson's drawings do to the usual machine diagram. Just as Heath Robinson ridicules absurd inventions, so does Saki burn up with the white flame of his scorn all pretenders to occult powers . . .[44]

Superstition and belief in the supernatural, after all, have always been anathema to the clear-thinking critic of society. Hence it should afford no surprise to the student of satire to discover Saki, like Hotspur, continually inveighing against the skimble-scramble hodgepodge of the Glendowers of the world. Which, however, is not to say that Munro himself does not often have recourse to unaccountable phenomena for the sake of plot interest.

Once again, moreover, the caution must be urged that Saki's humor has a certain fragility and evasiveness that one had best respect. Humor must not professedly teach, and it must not professedly preach, but it must do both if it would live forever. Saki's humor, we are convinced, does both to a considerable extent. The humorists, furthermore, who contribute pleasure to a wide audience are the ones who create characters and tell tales, the ones who are storytellers at heart. Saki was, if anything, a superlative storyteller. So far so good, but how pre-

---

[44] S. P. B. Mais, *op. cit.*, p. 323.

cisely are we to arrive at the quintessence that is Saki? We have already said something about his satire and his irony. It behooves us now to add some remarks about his humor as well as the nature of humor in general.

One of the things most commonly said about humorists is that they are really very melancholy people—clowns with breaking hearts. There is, of course, some truth in this. But qualification is necessary, especially in the case of Saki, who hardly strikes one as a weeping "comic" parading the pageant of his bleeding heart before the eyes of a harsh and cruel world. It could probably be more safely submitted that there is a strain of melancholy running through everyone's life, and that a humorist, more sensible of it than some others, compensates for it actively and positively. This certainly seems to fit the case of our author, whose air of self-sufficiency, nevertheless, must needs give us pause even here. For in his writing we constantly encounter a disdainful and condescending note that precludes not only sentimentalism but even laughter through tears. Munro can elicit indignation and raucous amusement but never empathy or sympathy. We may be terrified by his hero-villains and moved with a fascination akin to fear by their Iago-like machinations. Yet for their victims, if we do not join in the author's contempt, we feel only indifference. That is where Munro differs from the pure humorist like Ring Lardner or Stephen Leacock. He is, to be sure, often flippant, nonsensical, and "light," but the over-all effect of his humor is one of disillusioned negation and embittered dissatisfaction. Munro's humorous sallies are pungent with saline wit but are seldom cathartic. The reader, as often as not, finds himself laughing from the teeth out.

Munro's humor, we are led to conclude, is in many respects unique and peculiar to himself. At the same time, we recognize his affinity with other humorists by observing that its essence is the discovery and rejection of the absurd. For the humorist is very much in the position of the little girl who, having been reproached with some vehemence for kicking her kind nurse, said despairingly: "I can't kick Father, and I can't kick Mother, and I can't kick the baby. If I can't kick Nannie, whom am I to kick?" The incontrovertible fact is that someone has to be kicked, since "kicking" is not only a natural outlet for ill temper and a necessary corrective to nonsensical malfeasance, but also the foundation of much fun. This it is that the detractors of Saki must recognize. However viciously and wantonly he may "kick," his pedal blows are more often than not salutory, if not always decorous and tactful. Shock treatment is still sound psychiatric therapy. If we are sufficiently educated and sufficiently intelligent to think, our range of humor is wider than if we were less well endowed. Humor is a pleasure-giving device largely because it eludes reason; but in the apprehension of an aburdity through the working of the comic spirit there is a foundation of reason and an impetus to human companionship. That is why Saki has always had his eclectic public. His humor is as good an index as any to intelligence, and a sure guide to the enlightened understanding of a foolish humanity straying pitiably from paths where they might be happy.

The opening tale in Saki's third volume of short stories appropriately sets the tone of the whole. "The She-Wolf" recounts another instance in which the ever-present Clovis calls the bluff of a fatuous pretender to supernatural attainments. Leonard Bilsiter, whose aunt averred that she had actually seen him turn a vegetable marrow into a wood pigeon before her very eyes, proves an easy prey to the enterprise of Master Sangrail. With the gleeful collusion of Mary Hampton, who badgers Bilsiter to turn her into a she-wolf, and Lord Pabham, who among his collection of wild animals has a comparatively tame timber wolf, Louisa, Clovis has little difficulty in discomfiting and terrifying the obnoxious professor of Siberian magic.

At an auspicious moment during a house party, Mary disappears and Louisa stalks into the living room frightening everyone out of his wits. Bilsiter, of course, is too dumbfounded to claim the metamorphosis as his own. What is more, his reiterated disclaimer is met with a general murmur of impatient disbelief. When Mary suddenly reappears and questions him archly, he can only shake his head feebly. It is then that Clovis delivers the *coup de grâce* by claiming that it was he who effected the miraculous transformation:

> "It was I who took that liberty," said Clovis; "you see, I happen to have lived for a couple of years in North-eastern Russia, and I have more than a tourist's acquaintance with the magic craft of that region. One does not care to speak about these strange powers, but once in a while, when one hears a lot of nonsense being talked about them, one is tempted to show what Siberian magic can accomplish in the hands of some one who really understands it. I yielded to that temptation. May I have some brandy? The effect has left me rather faint."
>
> If Leonard Bilsiter could at this moment have transformed Clovis into a cockroach and then have stepped on him, he would gladly have performed both operations.[45]

"Laura" is a further excursion into the realm of the supernatural. The feminine appellation Laura, which is ever redolent of nostalgia and romantic vistas, can, alas, summon Saki only to a macabre treatment of reincarnation. The story is about a girl named Laura who, at the point of death, declares that she is coming back as an otter to worry her friends. She does so and in the process devours some of the choicest fowl of her friend, Amanda. Having been hunted down and killed in that capacity, she undauntedly reappears next in the guise of a naked, brown Nubian boy who tosses all the clean shirts of Egbert, Amanda's husband, into the bath of a Cairo hotel. It is perfectly understandable that after this train of unusual events, Amanda falls prey to nervous prostration.

---

[45] *S. S.*, p. 273.

"The Boar-Pig" is a descent into the bathetic and tells of Mrs. Philidore Stossen and her daughter, who were thwarted in their desire to "crash" a garden party by a Yorkshire boar-pig that had been set loose with malice aforethought by the young daughter of the hostess, Matilda Cuvering. The pig's name, anticlimactically enough, was Tarquin.

"The Brogue," the story of a recalcitrant horse that is inadvertently sold to a man who is about to propose to one of the daughters of the seller, is disappointing, although the wit of Clovis saves it from a blanket condemnation.

And the same applies to "The Hen." Here Clovis obliges his mother by getting rid of a lady guest whose arch female enemy is about to visit the Sangrails. He accomplishes this task very adroitly by telling her that their family butler has delusions, and that his present one is that she is Queen Anne, and, therefore, ought to be properly dead.

All of these first five tales, in fact, are vastly inferior to the best of Saki. "The Open Window," however, although certainly not among the best, is a justly celebrated one, often anthologized. In it we again have the stock Saki situation in which an adolescent perpetrates a hoax on a gullible grownup. The victim in this instance is Framton Nuttel, who migrates to a rural retreat for some rest and quiet. At the insistence of a city aunt, he goes to call on one of her rural acquaintances, and thereon hangs the tale that is worth rehearsing:

> "My aunt will be down presently, Mr. Nuttel," said a very self-possessed young lady of fifteen . . .
>
> "Her great tragedy happened just three years ago . . .
>
> "You may wonder why we keep that window wide open on an October afternoon . . .
>
> "Out through that window, three years ago to a day, her husband and her two young brothers went off for their day's shooting. They never came back . . . Poor aunt always thinks that they will come back some day . . . That is why the window is kept open every evening till it is dusk . . ."

It was a relief to Framton, when the aunt bustled into the room with a whirl of apologies for being late . . .

"I hope you don't mind the open window," she said briskly; "my husband and brothers will be home directly from shooting . . ."

She rattled on cheerfully . . . To Framton it was all purely horrible . . .

"Here they are at last!" she cried. "Just in time for tea, and don't they look as if they were muddy up to the eyes!"

Framton shivered slightly and turned towards the niece with a look intended to convey sympathetic comprehension. The child was staring out through the open window with dazed horror in her eyes. In a chill shock of nameless fear Framton swung round in his seat and looked in the same direction.

In the deepening twilight three figures were walking across the lawn towards the window . . .

Framton grabbed wildly at his stick and hat; the hall-door, the gravel-drive, and the front gate were dimly noted stages in his headlong retreat. A cyclist coming along the road had to run into the hedge to avoid imminent collision . . .

"A most extraordinary man . . . Mr. Nuttel," said Mrs. Sappleton. . . ."One would think he had seen a ghost."

"I expect it was the spaniel," said the niece calmly . . .[46]

This, for a change, is pure, unadulterated humor, with no trace whatever of acerbity or bitter almonds. We are heartily amused and we find the laughter not at all painful. Even Saki's abrasive irony is conspicuous by its absence.

But not for long. Irony reappears in "The Treasure-Ship," where the Duchess of Dulverton, although accounted wealthy in the world's eyes, seeks to enhance her financial status by promoting a scheme for recovering the treasure of an ancient, sunken galleon. To head this expedition in deep-sea diving, she appoints a poor relation, a nephew named Vasco Honiton:

The name Vasco had been given him possibly in the hope that he might live up to its adventurous tradition, but he limited himself strictly to the home industry of adventurer, preferring

─────────
46 *Ibid.*, pp. 294–97.

to exploit the assured rather than to explore the unknown. Lulu's intercourse with him had been restricted of recent years to the negative processes of being out of town when he called on her, and short of money when he wrote her.[47]

She allows him three weeks in which to test everything thoroughly before starting on the treasure hunt. At the expiration of the allotted time, Vasco reports promptly to his aunt on his progress. The dialogue is too exquisitely and happily phrased to permit of wanton digestion:

"The apparatus works beautifully," he informed his aunt . . . "We found something in the way of a sunken wreck . . ."

"A wreck in Innisgluther Bay!" exclaimed Lulu.

"A submerged motor-boat, the *Sub-Rosa*," said Vasco.

"No, really?" said Lulu; "poor Billy Yuttley's boat. I remember it went down somewhere off that coast some three years ago . . . People said at the time that the boat was capsized intentionally —a case of suicide, you know . . ."

"In this case they were right," said Vasco.

"What do you mean?" asked the Duchess hurriedly.

"I know," said Vasco simply.

"Know? How can you know? . . ."

"In a locker of the *Sub-Rosa* I found a watertight strongbox. It contained papers . . ." He drew out a folded slip of paper. The Duchess snatched at it in almost indecent haste . . .

"Was this in the *Sub-Rosa's* strongbox?" she asked.

"Oh, no," said Vasco carelessly, "that is a list of the well-known people who should be involved in a very disagreeable scandal if the *Sub-Rosa's* papers were made public . . ."

The Duchess gazed helplessly at the string of names . . . As a matter of fact, her own name at the head of the list exercised an almost paralysing effect on her thinking faculties . . .

Lulu glared at her nephew for some moments in silence. Then she asked hoarsely: "What are you going to do?"

"Nothing — for the remainder of my life," he answered meaningly . . .

Lulu's relative, who lived at the Court of Monaco, got quite

47 *Ibid.*, p. 299.

a snappish answer when she wrote recommending some further invention in the realm of marine research.[48]

The situation that paves the way for the delicious humor and delectable irony in this instance is the purely conventional one in which a Volpone or an Iago overreaches himself. It is one that Saki has recourse to over and over again. It is the "machinery" of a large number of his tales and sketches, which, were it not for the exotic beings who inhabit them and who converse with a studied flippancy and a deliberative understatement, would put one instantaneously in mind of the homiletic *exempla* of the medieval ages. From the days of the incomparable Scheherazade and Boccaccio and Chaucer, the indefatigable spinners of yarns have never tired of edifying us with the universal truths that the Goddess Fortuna does not like too full a fortune, and that *radix malorum est cupiditas.* But whereas the Greek tragedians exploit the irony that inheres in the dramatic psychology of hubris, the calm confidence and the self-assured arrogance that precede a fall, Saki, eschewing the excitation of pity, albeit not terror, contents himself with the spectacle of the embarrassing discomfiture of the overworldly at the hands of precocious adolescent Machiavels. And this difference in his ironic treatment of hypocrisy and deception bears careful scrutiny. Saki's is, of course, not the tragic irony of Sophocles or Shakespeare. Nor is it the deadly-earnest and animus-ridden irony of Swift in "A Modest Proposal." It contains a great deal of the sardonic and much of the dry mockery of the smilingly bitter *Rubaiyat* from which H. H. Munro took his pseudonym. What is even more important, if we are to explain why Saki is not among the first-rank satirists, is that his withering scorn is an end in itself and not seriously concerned with effecting reform or preaching sermons. In his tales and sketches we are never edified by seeing absolute good triumph over abso-

---

[48] *Ibid.,* pp. 300–301.

lute evil. We never find the satisfaction derived from the un-masking of vice by virtue or the exposure of deceit by honesty. Often as not, Saki's agent of correction, *der grosse Maschinist* —a Reginald or a Clovis or a juvenile delinquent—has no more claim to moral virtue than those whose turpitudes and pecca-dilloes he lays bare. If Shakespeare's *Othello* were to be seen from Saki's point of view, it would take shape as one great hoax after another, and the malignity of the villain would ap-pear as the cleverness and wittiness of a young man (Iago is twenty-eight) à la Clovis. Saki's "heroes" have much in com-mon with Volpone, although they lack the depth of that Eliza-bethan hero-villain. But Jonson, at least, makes certain that his protagonist receives his just deserts in the end, whereas Saki's Clovis continues to receive his creator's approbation with each newly hatched and imperturbably executed prank. And this boyish insensitiveness, this refined boorishness, this exasperat-ing aloofness, this Sakian trick of thwarting expectation, not only preclude attributing to him the supreme mastery of the *conte,* but also deny him the laurel of a great satirist. High com-edy is always serious. To laugh and by laughter be reformed is always admirable.

Yet Saki has one quality in common with great writers: a personal constancy, a slant of the mind that is as authentically Saki as other slants of the mind are Marvell, or Proust, or Gogol. It is important to remember that this element of personal constancy—call it individuality or flavor or originality or what you will—is not contaminated but reinforced by responsiveness to national or temporal influence. Marvell, without the meta-physical conceit that was the intellectual climate of his epoch, would be a lesser Marvell. The morbid and obsessive introver-sion of Proust transferred to Periclean Athens would not be great art at all; it would be a fiasco. And a Gogol un-Russian-ized would be like a Faulkner with the sentence structure of a Hemingway. Similarly, Saki's personal constancy is conditioned by constancy to his time and country. The peculiar and disdainful imperturbability that makes his style a refusal to be flustered or surprised or emphatic is the Sakian rendering of a national code of behavior, *le phlegme anglais*. But this imperturbability is exhibited against a background of the most unlikely events and unusual absurdities. For in that period of accustomed peace and prosperity, that calm in a teacup, prewar England, if one were to be imperturbable with any credit, one had to provide something a little more exigent than the ordinary material for perturbation. The truth must be faced: if Saki's exotic choice of subject was often his strength, it was often his weakness; if his insensitiveness carried him through, at times, to victory, it brought him, at times, to defeat.

And nowhere, perhaps, is this truth brought home to the student more forcefully than in the last twenty-nine sketches and tales of the collection *Beasts and Super-Beasts*. Saki's delineation of human beings, his empathy for animals and children alike, do not falter. Yet his tediousness begins to tell and even his invention begins to lag. Were it not for several conspicuous oases amid an otherwise unrelieved aridity, one would be inclined to pass over these stories in merciful silence. Those that we would not willingly let die can be said, however, to save, if they do not necessarily enhance, Saki's reputation.

There is, for example, the story of the flapper who kept the parliamentary candidate from brooding over politics at night by committing to his care a gamecock and a pig, on the plea that the outhouses had been flooded owing to the bursting of the reservoir.[49] There is the story of the estranged Duke and Duchess who refuse to go to the divorce courts unless they receive reimbursement from the newspapers who are capitalizing on the publicity.[50] A delightful tale in Saki's lighter vein is that of the man in the train who always failed to capture the atten-

---

49 *Ibid.,* pp. 307–11.
50 *Ibid.,* pp. 312–16.

tion of any of his fellow passengers until, at the instigation of a friend, he launched the following at their heads:

> "I had six pullets out of a pen of seven killed by a snake yesterday afternoon . . . It fascinated them with its deadly, glittering eyes, one after the other, and struck them down while they stood helpless . . . The six dead birds were Minorcas; the seventh was a Houdan with a mop of feathers all over its eyes. It could hardly see the snake at all, so of course it wasn't mesmerized like the others. It just could see something wriggling on the ground, and went for it and pecked it to death.[51]

From that day Blenkinthrope's reputation as the Munchausen of the party was assured. What is more, he was constantly adding to his repertoire, having at last found the open-sesame to the telling of unbelievable tales. When the story of the pullets began to wane in interest, he told one of a tame otter that had a tank in the garden to swim in, and whined restlessly whenever the water-rate was over due. But Nemesis soon overtook him. His wife followed the example of her mother and great-grandaunt by dying immediately after making a "Death's Head Patience" work out. At last something truly untoward had actually happened in the humdrum existence of this ambitious concocter of believe-it-or-not romances. He wrote out the full story only to find that he was disbelieved in every quarter. "Not the right thing to be Munchausing in a time of sorrow" was the general verdict, and forlornly chastened by the debacle of his visions of widespread publicity, he sank once more to "small beer," to conversation about canaries, beetroot, and potatoes, a fallen and lonely man. Ah, *vanitas vanitatum!*

As for irony, we have enough and to spare in the story of how the family of Harrowcluff came to make the Honours List. Those who cannot understand the craze for popular hit tunes made up of inane, skimble-scamble doggerel, or who find it

---

[51] *Ibid.*, pp. 328–29.

impossible to accept the abstruse constructions foisted upon obscure, contemporary poetry, would find this narrative truly enlightening. Basset, at the age of thirty-one, is the apple of his father's eye in contrast to Lucas, who is, as is usually the case, misconstrued in his idleness. The former had returned to England after keeping open a trade route, pacifying a province, and enforcing respect upon the unruly inhabitants in imperialistic fashion and with the least possible expense. It was expected that Whitehall would take an instinctive liking to him. On the other hand, his elder half-brother was always feverishly engrossed in a hodgepodge of impossible futilities that alternately bore and exasperate the members of his family. Lucas was forever discovering ideas and making schemes that were "simply it." One day the inspiration seized upon him as he was dressing:

". . . it will be *the* thing in the next music-hall *revue*. All London will go mad over it. It's just a couplet; of course there will be other words, but they won't matter. Listen:

> Cousin Teresa takes out Caesar,
> Fido, Jack, and the big borzoi.

A lilting, catchy sort of refrain, you see, and big-drum business on the two syllables of bor-zoi. It's immense."[52]

It was. To the amazement of his family the song caught on; the name of Harrowcluff became more and more famous until at length, under the heading "Merit in Literature," Colonel Harrowcluff had the satisfaction of seeing his son's name in the List of Honours. But is wasn't Basset. *O tempora, o mores!*

Then, in the best Reginald manner, there is the story of Cyprian, who preferred to accompany his aunt on a shopping expedition without a hat and was seen by her at intervals to be pocketing the money for various articles from buyers who mistook him for a salesman.[53] And in like vein we have the

---

[52] *Ibid.*, p. 349.
[53] *Ibid.*, pp. 369–70.

story of the young man who, having gambled all his own possessions, staked his mother's peerless cook, and lost.[54]

"The Story-Teller," in which Munro shows his understanding of child psychology, ought to be of inestimable value to those who want to know how to hold the attention of small boys and girls. The flick of the satiric whip at the end, when the aunt rebukes the stranger's self-volunteered fable as "improper," is delightful:

> "Unhappy woman!" he observed to himself as he walked down the platform of Templecombe station; "for the next six months or so those children will assail her in public with demands for an improper story!"[55]

In more savage and somber vein we have "The Romancers" and "The Schartz-Metterklume Method." The former is a downright example of perverted humor, in which a young blade tantalizingly raises the hopes of a down-and-out tramp and then suddenly leaves him without even the price of a cup of soup. The latter is a blunt satire against pedagogues and theories of education—topics that always receive biting sarcasm from an author who felt adults did not understand children. Saki also manages to score off the dominating female here, and in Lady Carlotta, the female counterpart to Clovis, and Mrs. Quabarl, the martinet mother, we have two wonderfully and perfectly realized women.

"Fur" is a wonderful study of the spiteful cattishness of women, and refutes those who would have us believe that Munro did not understand human beings and the motives that animate them. And the same may be said of "The Philanthropist and the Happy Cat," a study worthy of Balzac in its delineation of the false rationalization that leads a woman to think she is serenely and graciously happy. Jocantha Bessbury thinks that she

---

[54] *Ibid.*, p. 382.
[55] *Ibid.*, p. 402.

lacks for nothing until she feels philanthropic stirrings in her breast for an underprivileged, handsome youth whose eye, alas, she cannot catch. After this her husband and home begin to pall on her, and she envies her cat's imperturbable contentment. After reading a story like this one regrets that Saki, for some inexplicable reason, carefully skirted stories dealing intimately with affairs of the heart. It seems that had he so desired he might have rivaled Katherine Mansfield in this respect. Miss Ethel Munro has pointed out his reluctance to treat of love or sex. (See Appendix.)

But perhaps the best answer is provided by Saki himself in an unusual story called "The Mappined Life." This story instances, we believe, one of those rare occasions when Munro speaks *in propria persona.* And it is significant that in so doing he reveals a great deal of that anguish which the disillusioned idealist feels on such occasions. One catches overtones of Lucretius, Chekhov, and Fromm, when Munro writes:

> ". . . we are able to live our unreal, stupid little lives on our particular Mappin terrace, and persuade ourselves that we really are untrammelled men and women leading a reasonable existence in a reasonable sphere . . . we are trammelled . . . by restrictions of income and opportunity, and above all by lack of initiative . . . It's the dreadful little everyday acts of pretended importance that give the Mappin stamp to our life . . . nearly everything . . . is conventional make-believe."[56]

The thought here is as original and jejune as Pope's *Essay on Man.* However, it is not the thought itself so much as the insight we gain through the thought that should give us pause. For here, assuredly, we have the open-sesame to Saki's secret. At last the elusive Victorian Democritus stands before us unmasked. Underneath the satirist, ironist, and humorist, we discover what we already suspected: namely, the embittered jester, the disillusioned clown, the British Scaramouche, the passionate,

---

[56] *Ibid.,* pp. 544–46.

Byronic rebel against convention and hypocritical restraint. We perceive that Munro so loved life and spontaneity that he was out of all patience with the routine imposed upon man as a social being by a benighted and unimaginative society. The reason his favorite companions of this world were the Reginalds and the Clovises was that they, at least, would never grow up and worship at the shrine of routine. That explains his amazing empathy with children, who represented to him the only uninhibited and honest members of our regimented society. The enigmatic phenomenon of Saki, in fact, reduces to a very simple formula: Munro was a Victorian in revolt against Victorianism. The sadistic, the exaggerated, the grotesque, the mirth-provoking components of his work represent the iconoclastic lava of his irrepressible imagination. The verbally brilliant, polished, and cold expression and style of his work represent the artistic transformation of this lava into a literary achievement of no mean proportions. But at times, even in Saki, righteous indignation will break through as it does when the Fiend-Orator in "The Infernal Parliament" exclaims:

"Vices which are exclusively or predominatingly human are unblushingly described as inhuman, and, what is even more contemptible and ungenerous, as fiendish."[57]

This might well serve as a motto for Munro's short stories and sketches, which forever bring home to us the inherent perversity and mendacity of human beings. Munro proves objectionable only to those who are unwilling to confess to the truth of the Field-Orator's statement. But then, they are precisely the ones for whom Munro reserves his most savage indignation and invective. Swift told man to go to the Houyhnhnms for instruction; Munro, writing in an identical vein, directs their steps to the cat for instruction in courage and self-respect:

Confront a child, a puppy, and a kitten with a sudden danger;

57 *Ibid.*, p. 623.

the child will turn instinctively for assistance, the puppy will grovel in abject submission to the impending visitation, the kitten will brace its tiny body for a frantic resistance. And disassociate the luxury-loving cat from the atmosphere of social comfort in which it usually contrives to move, and observe it critically under the adverse conditions of civilization—that civilization which can impel a man to the degradation of clothing himself in tawdry ribald garments and capering mountebank dances in the streets for the earning of the few coins that keep him on the respectable, or non-criminal, side of society. The cat of the slums and alleys, starved, outcast, harried, still keeps amid the prowlings of its adversity the bold, free, panther-tread with which it paced of yore the temple courts of Thebes, still displays the self-reliant watchfulness which man has never taught it to lay aside. And when its shifts and clever managings have not sufficed to stave off inexorable fate, when its enemies have proved too strong or too many for its defensive powers, it dies fighting to the last, quivering with the choking rage of mastered resistance, and voicing in its death-yell that agony of bitter remonstrance which human animals, too, have flung at the powers that may be; the last protest against a destiny that might have made them happy—and has not.[58]

There is more than the mere love of animals revealed here, although that is present also. More important, however, we discover Saki in his full, satiric panoply. As in the fourth book of *Gulliver's Travels,* Munro, eschewing the umbrage of irony or humor, lashes out in unrestrained fury against the "damned, mangy human race." True, he never descended to the embittered and unrelenting pessimism of Twain's later years. But nowhere is his affinity to the American humorist and satirist more clear than here. Munro lacked the breadth and sweep of Twain, just as he was deficient in the enthralling humanity of the American novelist. But in temperament they were very much alike, and if Munro had sacrificed some of his polish in the cause of earthiness, he might have merited and claimed comparison on behalf of his Clovis and Reginald with Huck Finn and Tom Sawyer.

---

[58] *Ibid.,* pp. 626–27.

But for all his skill and fastidious choice of subject and treatment, he cannot rank among the great. His ambition, it seems, was to do well and not to do superlatively. And perhaps no higher tribute can be paid him than to say he did all the better for that. In his own genre, that of the Sakian short story, he is unexcelled and without peer.

Munro's last two collections of short stories, *The Toys of Peace* (1923) and *The Square Egg* (1924), published posthumously, are not as sustainedly successful as his earlier collections. To be sure, the ingredients—satire, irony, and humor, in pure or adulterated or inimitably blended form—are the same. What is more, stylistically these later Saki creations are, if possible, more flawless and maddeningly suave than those that preceded them. The narrative fabric is as translucent as ever, yet still surprisingly resilient and durable. But the over-all impression is one of mellowed and resigned wearisomeness. It is evident that the *tedium vitae* inheres not only in the informing tone of the stories but in the author himself. S. P. B. Mais ventures the suggestion that Munro was so ardently engrossed in the art of being a soldier, at this time, that writing must have seemed but toying with life and a sorry substitute for "the real thing."[59] In any event, there is no mistaking the frequent disarticulation of the narrative web and the enervation of motive tension consequent upon it. What is even more noticeable is the absence of that pungency and that dancing and saline malice that are so much an integral part of the earlier Saki. In one important respect, however, there is no marked "falling off"; Saki's perspicacity in dissecting and immolating, at one and the same time, the petty considerations of human conduct is as unsparing as ever. Since the perennials of the former collections —the ogreish adolescents, the dreadful aunts, the wolves, and

[59] Mais, *op. cit.*, p. 326.

Clovis—although not absent, are in the background, the author devotes more time to characterization, and editorial comment claims a larger share of the whole. We have fewer glittering epigrams and more sober reflections on life. And although these later stories may strike the reader as being less "sensational" and hardly as memorable as those that went before, nevertheless, by the same token, it will be apparent that they are more credible and less strained. Whatever one may deny Saki, one cannot deny him an unexampled facility and a felicity of phrase and expression.

The first story in *The Toys of Peace,* which gives its title to the collection of thirty-three tales, evinces clearly the author's preoccupation with war. Again Saki portrays discerningly the innate cruelty and instinctive sadism of children. The plot is inconsequential, and as is usually the case, the irony is occasioned and pointed by showing the adults coming out second best in a tussle of wills with the children. Eleanor Bope, being of a pacific turn of mind, induces her brother Harvey, albeit against his better judgment, to cooperate with her in indoctrinating her children in the notion that the arts of peace are infinitely superior to the arts of war. In concert, they seek to divert the children's taste from blood lust to the constructive pleasures of peace, from guns to ploughs, from toy soldiers to toy city councilors. Their uncle presents them on Easter with "toys of peace" —figures supposed to represent Mrs. Hemans, John Stuart Mill, and models of the Manchester branch of the Y.W.C.A. The result can be readily guessed; it is the typical Sakian fiasco:

> Peeping in through the doorway Harvey observed that the municipal dust-bin had been pierced with holes to accommodate the muzzles of imaginary cannon, and now represented the principal fortified position in Manchester; John Stuart Mill had been dipped in red ink, and apparently stood for Marshal Saxe.
>
> Louis orders his troops to surround the Young Women's Christian Association and seize the lot of them.
>
> "Once back at the Louvre and the girls are mine," he ex-

claims. "We must use Mrs. Hemans again for one of the girls; she says 'Never,' and stabs Marshal Saxe to the heart."[60]

One cannot help being reminded of Swift's war-minded Lilliputians and the glowing account of gunpowder that Gulliver presents to the Brobdingnagian monarch. Saki's children, in fact, seem to serve the same function in the author's view of life and society as do the pygmies in the first book of *Gulliver's Travels:* at one remove from the adult and actual world, they present its refined cruelty and turpitude in the unique Sakian realm, where these failings appear not only heinous but infantile and ludicrous as well. This is where many critics who feel Saki hated children have gone astray. Saki's psychology of childhood, as we have said before, is profound. He did not detest and recoil from children as Swift did; nor was he inclined to sentimentalize them as did Hugo and Dickens. Saki's children closely resemble Shakespeare's Puck; they are mischievous and hell-bent imps who delight in vexing those fools called mortals. Theirs is not the "innocence" of Blake but rather the "experience" of Gide.

But children are relegated to the background in these later stories of Munro. Adults with their petty inanities predominate. There is, for example, Jane Thropplestance, who was so absentminded that one day she forgot where she mislaid her niece.[61] There is James Cushat-Prinkly, who discovers what all bachelors should never permit themselves to forget: namely, that the "little woman" always is metamorphosed into a different woman after the honeymoon is over.[62] More versed in the ways of tyrannizing wives is Strudwarden, who gains the ascendancy over his capricious spouse by the simple expedient of destroying a lifelike imitation of a toy Pomeranian that she had for months passed off as a live animal, whose whims she placed above the demands of her husband:

---

[60] *S. S.*, p. 450.   [61] *Ibid.*, pp. 450–53.   [62] *Ibid.*, pp. 454–58.

"Louis is dead . . . he flew at the butcher-boy and bit him, and he bit me too, when I tried to get him off, so I had to have him destroyed. You warned me that he snapped, but you didn't tell me that he was downright dangerous. I shall have to pay the boy something heavy by way of compensation, so you will have to go without those buckles that you wanted to have for Easter; also I shall have to go to Vienna to consult Dr. Schroeder, who is a specialist on dog-bites, and you will have to come too. I have sent what remains of Louis to Rowland Ward to be stuffed; that will be my Easter gift to you instead of the buckles . . ."

Lena Strudwarden did not weep, but her attempt at laughing was an unmistakable failure.[63]

The pat moral of which is that there are more ways than one of taming a shrew.

It is a pity Munro never married. What an experience he would have been for his wife. Although no woman hater like Swift, Munro was very much like Shaw in seeing through the wiles of man's "lovely bane," and, as already stated, we regret that his stories bear the extreme, Victorian stamp of emasculation. His women are seldom if ever of the heroine mold. The hostile portraits are essentially prototypes of Philip Wylie's "moms." For that very reason, however, they are very like women as bachelors feel they know them—brazen, self-sufficient, predatory, loquacious, and impossible.

Take, as a moot illustration, Matilda, who has to house a bishop with whom she is not on speaking terms. As chance would have it, the Gwadlipichee chose to overflow its banks at this inopportune time. What ensues is of rare vintage, even as Sakian dialogues go. The narrator is Matilda:

"I'm afraid there is nowhere for you to sit," I said coldly; "the verandah is full of goats."

"There is a goat in my bedroom," he observed with equal coldness, and more than a suspicion of sardonic reproach.

---

[63] *Ibid.*, p. 473.

"Really," I said, "another survivor! I thought all the other goats were done for."

"This particular goat is quite done for," he said; "it is being devoured by a leopard at the present moment. That is why I left the room; some animals resent being watched while they are eating."[64]

The only trouble here is that Matilda sounds very much as would Clovis Sangrail, that "spiced" gentleman of leisure, on a similar occasion.

In the last analysis, it is not so much the puppets—be they men or women—who count as the puppet master whose genius is never romantically sweet or sentimentally mellow. The excitement of Saki is an irritating one, which pains like a dentist's drill on an exposed nerve.

> He surprises us [writes Mais], just as "O. Henry" surprises us by turning a complete somersault in his last sentences after astonishing us with all manner of gymnastic capers in each paragraph before. It reminds one of music-hall acrobats who, after taking our breath away several times during their "turn," make their adieux by performing some incredible antic that leaves us too shattered even to applaud.[65]

Less intent than O. Henry on twisting the story's tale, he is past master of that device when he chooses. And this consideration leads to another: Why does Saki so frequently have recourse to hoaxes for his plots? Why does he take an almost Iago-like satisfaction in those of his characters who are fluent liars, who exercise their nimble wits at the discomfiture of others? Why is an amiable soul like Octavian Ruttle shamelessly ridiculed by the terror tactics of three diabolical children?[66] We have sought elsewhere to provide answers and explanations to these questions.

---

[64] *Ibid.*, pp. 476–77.
[65] Mais, *op. cit.*, p. 329.
[66] *S. S.*, pp. 478–84.

CHAPTER III

The Novels

This story has no moral. If it points out an evil at any rate it suggests no remedy.[1]

ALTHOUGH Saki's forte is confessedly the short story, his two excursions into the realm of the novel cannot be dismissed lightly. They are by no means great novels, but they are important novels, and merit much more praise than anyone has thus far been willing to bestow on them. Moreover, they appear to have been more seriously and more deeply felt, even though here, also, Saki's elegances tended to be hard and crystalline rather than malleable. Saki possessed the inventive powers of a great novelist, and, had he lived, might have produced a novel that the world would not willingly let die. But he lacked the imaginative sweep and sustained penetration of the masters. Like Jane Austen, he knew enough to restrict himself to the society and types of characters with whom he had a firsthand acquaintance. But unlike Austen, he was not genius enough to rise above his limitations. The plot machinery creaks awkwardly in many places, and there are not enough compensatory excellences in Saki, as there are in Hardy, to make us forget strained coincidences and clumsy foreshadowing. Yet despite their flaws, his novels are the most artistically executed of his works. His style and diction are precise, meticulous, and scintillating. And

---

[1] H. H. Munro, *The Unbearable Bassington.*

the characterization never falters in the deftness and sureness
of his strokes. Saki's irony is as mordant as ever, and the epigrams come thick and fast. His vein of macabre, supernatural
fantasy lends atmosphere, and his grim cruelty provides a pi-
quancy that is not entirely unpleasant.

This is especially true of *The Unbearable Bassington* (1912),
a satiric work adorned with gloom, epigrams, bitter jokes, and
the irony of fate. Written at a time when sociology was being
promulgated from the stage, it renders the bridge-playing class-
es, as they were, with power and with no "repertory" dullness.
It is clever, brilliant, ironic, witty, somber, elegant, and grim.
The characterization is telling and effective. Comus Bassington
is a typical Sakian playboy—an unfortunate, embittered Clovis.
Estranged from society, his mother, and his sweetheart, he is
ultimately destroyed by his willfulness, recklessness, and irresponsibility. Francesca, his mother, is, in our humble opinion,
the most brilliant characterization in all of Saki. She attains
true tragic proportions and is the only Sakian character for
whom we ever feel any sympathy.

There may be those who will disagree, but we feel that at
no time does Francesca deserve condemnation. To us she is
much more sympathetic than Comus. The twentieth century's
preoccupation with the Oedipus complex in fiction has led to
many deplorable studies in which no sympathy whatever is ac-
corded the mother, and in which the reader is asked to condemn
her unequivocally. This is not only a heinous travesty of the
sacredness of parental love, but a nearsighted and too frequently
specious misunderstanding of Freud. It is significant in this con-
nection to recall that the most excellent treatment of mother
love, that of D. H. Lawrence in *Sons and Lovers,* is, on the
whole, a sympathetic portrayal of Mrs. Morel, the mother. And
so is that of Francesca, whether Saki intended it or not.

Nothing is too bad for Comus. Saki's attempt to heighten
the sense of impending tragedy by ominous omens is entirely

unworthy of the great novelist. It is too obvious and one is conscious of the disparity existing in this respect between Munro and, say, Conrad or Mann. What is more, it fails completely in what its author no doubt intended—to make us feel pity for Comus.

Here is where we detect a fundamental flaw in Saki's understanding of human nature. For although we may tolerate the Falstaffs of the world simply because they amuse us and help while away our idle moments, we do not hesitate for a moment in rejecting them when expediency demands it. Sir John was right; we *do* hate their youth when it becomes mere adolescent irresponsibility. This is something Munro simply couldn't grasp: namely, that a Reginald or a Clovis has no place in a serious and realistic portrayal of life.

The suspicion that there is a great deal of Munro in Comus merely substantiates our argument. For to the extent that Comus is Munro, to that extent are we able to appreciate that vague feeling of ambiguous hurt that permeates all of Saki's short stories, despite the mask of *sang-froid* and urbanity to be found on their surface. It will be recalled that, for all his arrogance and air of being above it all, we detected a note of real bitterness in such stories as "The Mappined Life"—evidence that Saki was, at bottom, something less comfortable than a lighthearted and irresponsible humorist. Amid his shimmering epigrams, amid his verbal dexterity, amid his insouciance, we are ever aware of an underlying malaise, or, at the least, of a deep-seated uneasiness.

In both *The Unbearable Bassington* and *When William Came,* though the core be tragedy, we have the same blending of seriousness and flippancy conducive to a hollow, Prufrock-like effect. What is more, we find Saki to be much more of a sentimentalist, and much more a typical product of his class and its prejudices, than we would have normally expected in one so gay, debonair, and intractable. But perhaps the novels should be permitted to speak for themselves. They do this admirably.

The first in order of composition is the story of a young man, the only son of a widowed mother. He is a wastrel pure and simple; he has the charm of a stoat or a weasel—animals considered vermin by all right-thinking British gentlemen. His nature and proclivities are admirably summed up by two of his schoolmasters:

> "Nonsense; boys are Nature's raw material."
> "Millions of boys are. There are just a few, and Bassington is one of them, who are Nature's highly finished product when they are in the schoolboy stage, and we, who are supposed to be moulding raw material, are quite helpless when we come in contact with them."
> "But what happens to them when they grow up?"
> "They never do grow up," said the housemaster; "that is their tragedy. Bassington will certainly never grow out of his present stage."[2]

Bassington didn't; nor, for that matter, did Munro, in his writings at least, despite the fact that self-knowledge is the earmark of maturity. But of what avail is self-knowledge if one rebels against it? Witness Wilde and Byron. Maurice Baring put his finger on the source of the trouble when he wrote:

> Comus sometimes talks, dreams, improvises, jokes, revels in the manner of Peter Pan, *but he does not think in the manner of Peter Pan.* And this contradiction and conjunction of opposites make for tragedy.[3]

Comus is his own dearest enemy, and in the first part of the novel, Saki is not inclined to mince matters when it comes to dissecting his weakness:

> In an animal world, and a fiercely competitive animal world at that, something more was needed than the decorative *abandon* of

---

[2] H. H. Munro, *The Novels and Plays of Saki* (London, 1949), p. 22. Hereafter *Novels and Plays.*
[3] In his introduction to *The Unbearable Bassington, Novels and Plays,* p. 6.

the field lily, and it was just that something more which Comus
seemed unable or unwilling to provide on his own account; it was
just the lack of that something more which left him sulking with
Fate over the numerous break-downs and stumbling-blocks that
held him up on what he expected to be a triumphal or, at any
rate, unimpeded progress.[4]

When he might marry an heiress and recoup his losses as
well as insure his future, he estranges her affections by borrow-
ing money from her. Elaine de Frey loves him, and she does not
love her money; but she cannot run counter to the traditional
opinion that young men who "sponge" are not good prospective husbands. There is one wrong that a woman can never for-
give—lack of consideration. And it is in that department that
Comus particularly antagonizes her. He nettles her by abscond-
ing with her silver butter dish, half in jest, to be sure, but at an
extremely inopportune moment, when she is not in the mood for
jesting. Then, while she is still ruffled, he asks her for a small
loan, which incenses her beyond all measure—not so much because she minds his impecuniousness but because he strikes her
as callous and shameless. It is this episode that precipitates her
into the arms of Courtenay Youghal, whom she does not love
but, nevertheless, marries out of pique. The entire "business"
is handled very capably by Saki, who gives us to understand that
in rejecting Comus she not only makes herself miserable but
seals that young man's doom as well. For his mother cannot but
view his failure in the matrimonial market as the last straw.

Francesca, like Elaine, loves Comus, but she does not love
supporting him:

> Francesca was, in her own way, fonder of Comus than of any
> one else in the world, and if he had been browning his skin some-
> where east of Suez she would probably have kissed his photograph
> with genuine fervour every night before going to bed . . . But with
> the best-beloved installed under her roof, occupying an unreason-
> able amount of cubic space, and demanding daily sacrifices instead

---

[4] *Novels and Plays,* pp. 32–33.

of providing the raw material for one, her feelings were tinged
with irritation rather than affection.[5]

It is perfectly understandable that she was not prepared to sell
her Van der Meulen in order to have the dubious pleasure of
the society of someone who ate more than his fair share of
plovers' eggs. So, after his fiasco with Elaine, his mother with
quick determination insists on shipping him off to Africa, even
though she fears she is sending him to his death. Comus's protest is not so much desperate as it is perfunctory:

> "Can't we sell something?" asked Comus.
> He made no actual suggestion as to what should be sacrificed,
> but he was looking straight at the Van der Meulen.
> For a moment Francesca felt a stifling sensation of weakness, as
> though her heart was going to stop beating. Then she sat forward
> in her chair and spoke with energy, almost fierceness.
> "When I am dead my things can be sold and dispersed. As long
> as I am alive I prefer to keep them by me."[6]

And so he is packed off to Africa, where he is miserable and
where he dies of a fever. Happily the story does not end with
a conventional *requiescat in pace*. For it is in that fate of the
mother that we experience the real tragic emotion.

It is in portraying Francesca's realization, when it is too
late, that her zealously guarded possessions do not matter that
Munro really excels himself. Her attainment to this self-knowledge is not unlike the recognition scene in classical Greek tragedy. Moreover, like Oedipus, Francesca does not die; hers is the
greater agony of having to live on knowing what she knows.

She is first introduced to us as one who, if asked, in an un-
guarded moment, to describe herself, would probably have
described her drawing-room. The Greek *moira* (Fate) seems to
have marked her down, as well as her son, for suffering:

---

[5] *Ibid.,* p. 33.
[6] *Ibid.,* p. 105.

> Francesca was one of those women towards whom Fate appears
> to have the best intentions and never to carry them into practice.[7]

Although not soured by the vicissitudes of fortune, she has learned to moderate her enthusiasms and to employ her cherished drawing-room acquisitions as a buffer to the vexations of daily existence. And it is, of course, the great Van der Meulen that had come from her father's home as part of her wedding dowry that she prizes most of all. It is this treasure that ultimately assumes, in Saki's novel, the tragic proportions of Othello's handkerchief.

Her son, of course, is a great trial to her, but she always bears up courageously, even in the face of his most insufferable provocations. Nor is there any doubt that she is genuinely grieved at his departure. Clairvoyantly, as soon as she receives the first telegram informing her he is stricken, she knows he will die:

> She knew that she would never see Comus again, and she knew that she loved him beyond all things that the world could hold for her. It was no sudden rush of pity or compunction that clouded her judgment or gilded her recollection of him; she saw him as he was, the beautiful wayward laughing boy, with his naughtiness, his exasperating selfishness, his insurmountable folly and perverseness, his cruelty that spared not even himself, as he was, as he always had been, she knew that he was the one thing that the Fates had willed that she should love.[8]

In the splendidly moving last chapter of the novel, we see her go for a walk in St. James's Park in an endeavor to put off the horrible moment when she knows she will have to open the second dreaded telegram reporting his death. There she meets Lady Caroline Benaresg who understands—at a glance—what she is waiting for:

> "I wish I could say something; I can't." Lady Caroline spoke in a harsh, grunting voice that few people had ever heard her use.[9]

---

[7] *Ibid.*, p. 11.   [8] *Ibid.*, p. 138.   [9] *Ibid.*, p. 141.

Francesca returns home and finds the fatal telegram awaiting her. The tragedy is almost completed—all but the final twist of the Sakian screw to which we have been habituated by the short stories. At this, the most tragic moment in her life, Francesca's brother drops in to tell her that an expert who had examined her Van der Meulen found it a copy. Not knowing of her bereavement, he mistakes the anguish in her eyes for disappointment at his announcement, and proceeds to console her. And all the while—

> Francesca sat in stricken silence, crushing the folded morsel of paper tightly in her hand and wondering if the thin, cheerful voice with its pitiless, ghastly mockery of consolation would never stop.[10]

This, we submit, is the best thing in the vein of irony that Saki ever did. There may be some who feel that this entire episode is superfluous, or that it would have been better if the picture had turned out to be genuine and she had given it away. But we cannot agree. The ending as it stands cannot be improved upon, and the irony to be found here is of a much higher order than that, say, in the short story "The Reticence of Lady Anne." The humorous irony of Chaucer in the "Book of the Duchess" is here transfigured into stark, tragic notes.

Munro assures us that the story has no moral. He is right. There are some stories too austere to have a moral. For the moral story is a form of vegetation that germinates only in a rather gross soil, requiring to be manured by a good deal of sentiment. And *The Unbearable Bassington* is not of this kind. Here the Sakian imperturbability masters something more serious than werewolves. The situation here is one in which three persons are doomed with classical precision to immolate themselves with their eyes open. Saki's study of the will to destruction latent in human nature, although not of so high an order as that of Hardy's in *The Mayor of Casterbridge* or Gide in *The*

---

10 *Ibid.*, p. 143.

Immoralist, is, nevertheless, a brilliant one. We see him rise from the pettish imperturbability of Clovis to something better: to restraint and objective detachment, to serious characterization and a criticism of life.

When William Came (1913) is a prophetic fantasy of an England vanquished by the Hohenzollerns. It is neither as entertaining nor as artistically satisfying as *The Unbearable Bassington.* Actually, one feels hesitant about even calling it a novel. It has a closer affinity with such diverse works as *Gulliver's Travels, Brave New World, It Can't Happen Here, The Disappearance,* and *Nineteen Eighty-four.* The end product may best be characterized as a hodgepodge comprised of satire, propaganda, and trenchant wit. But Munro is too much in earnest and too animus-ridden here to pay much attention to the niceties of artistic composition. His humor, of course, does not desert him, but it is altogether too evident that his view of the world has suddenly become painfully jaundiced. He takes himself too seriously, and although he had just grounds for doing so, we cannot help but feel that his work suffers from his pessimism. He leaves loose ends everywhere. Even in his forte, dialogue, delightful as it often is, funny as it nearly always is, we detect the distraught craftsman. Time and again, it becomes monologue judiciously fed, one character giving and the other taking. The ending is likewise disappointing. The tale breaks off abruptly with gloomy forebodings of the future. And though this may be realistic, we feel cheated, especially since Munro had accustomed us to superlative Parthian shots. A lame ending, in fact, is almost unforgivable in Saki.

This, however, is not to deny the work its merits, of which it has many. To the British public, of course, the writer's infectious love of his country is especially gratifying. The castigation of politics and politicians is never offensive when it is designed to make for national unity and strength. In fact, Saki,

wearing the guise of a bellicose jingo and hymning with fervor
the glories of British imperialism and the delights of English
hedges and hunting fields, is probably, on the whole, more
palatable to his countrymen than Saki as Clovis ridiculing Glad-
stonian society.

Which is by no means to imply that Saki the satirist is here
in complete abeyance. The novel, after all, is essentially a call
to arms. Munro is desirous of shocking his compeers out of their
lethargy and alarming complacency. Hence he is not unsparing
in the use of the rod of satirical castigation. His scorn for a
social world that submitted supinely to Hohenzollern domina-
tion, rather than sacrifice its petty vanities and pleasures, is as
eloquent and withering as one could ask. Nor should we over-
look the fact that his prophecy was, in a sense, apocalyptic.
Now, when we can examine his work in calm perspective, we
perceive the amazing insight Munro revealed in gauging the
danger that threatened his country before World War I. With
uncanny acumen, Munro pointed out the intrinsic speciousness
that inheres at bottom in all policies of pacifism in a world
dedicated to self-aggrandizement. In our own day and age, neither Sinclair Lewis nor George Orwell has phrased this universal truth with more unerring logic. In other words, the lesson
preached by Munro in *When William Came* is as timely today
as it was in the halcyon days of George V. It is indeed surprising that it has not occurred to the Saki enthusiasts to revive this
novel of their idol in the present day. If it is lacking in the sen-
sationalism of a Wylie or an Orwell, it is certainly not lacking
in the driving force of its arguments and convictions. Human
nature—if we may be permitted a truism—is a constant that
does not change with the innovations of each succeeding age.
It is not difficult, therefore, for the contemporary reader to
identify himself with the principals of Munro's fancy, even
though he may feel much removed from the social set depicted
by the author.

Two harrowing world conflicts have taught us the lesson Munro sought to disseminate in 1913: namely, that we must take *cum grano salis* the truth that peace at any cost is more honorable than war. We have gradually, albeit painfully, shed many of our preposterous hypocrisies that we were so fond of concealing beneath the euphemism "ideals." "Militarism" though still occasionally denounced in pulpits is a palpably otiose bugbear. The irony implicit in this state of affairs is of rare vintage, and it is a pity that Munro was completely oblivious to it. But then, Munro was no Swift.

It is not our primary intent, however, to present Munro's work as a grave essay in statecraft. The book, on the whole, remains in the realm of fancy. Munro still displays in abundance that unique and inimitable light touch that sets him apart from all other writers. Take, for example, the effortless opening of the novel, a glittering example of art that conceals art:

> Cicely Yeovil sat in a low swing chair, alternately looking at herself in a mirror and at the other occupant of the room in the flesh. Both prospects gave her undisguised satisfaction. Without being vain she was duly appreciative of good looks, whether in herself or in another, and the reflection that she saw in the mirror, and the young man whom she saw seated at the piano, would have come with credit out of a more severely critical inspection. Probably she looked longer and with greater appreciation at the piano-player than at her own image; her good looks were an inherited possession, that had been with her more or less all her life, while Ronnie Storre was a comparatively new acquisition, discovered and achieved, so to speak, by her own enterprise, selected by her own good taste. Fate had given her adorable eyelashes and an excellent profile. Ronnie was an indulgence she had bestowed on herself.[11]

One would have to search far and wide in the realm of gold —in Keatsian phrase—before one came upon a prose style as sedate, polished, impeccable, and pure as that of Munro. The words simply flow in mellifluous and unruffled tempo like the

---

[11] *Ibid.*, p. 153.

sparkling streams of water voided by an eighteenth-century fountain. His diction has the serenity of an Addison with the pungency of a Shaw.

Nor can it be said that his wit is any less flashing than of old. His gift for epigram is still in profuse evidence. Epigram making indulged in more for the sake of sound than sense, or for the fun of twisting phrases and juggling with words and syllables and antithesis may degenerate into mere verbalism. And Saki cannot be said to be entirely free from this charge of verbalism. But more often than not he rises perceptibly above it, as in the following:

> "While life is with us how little of life even the materialist understands."[12]
> "Love is one of the few things in which the make-believe is superior to the genuine, it lasts longer, and you get more fun out of it, and it's easier to replace when you've done with it."[13]

In less good taste, we have the following:

> "A husband with asthma is like a captive golf-ball, you can always put your hand on him when you want him."[14]

We even have pure humor, although it is somewhat strained and lacks spontaneity. Perhaps the best example of it—spiced as ever with the inevitable dram of Sakian malice—may be found in the press notice commenting on the performance of Gorla Mustelford at the Caravansary. Gorla's debut was sponsored by Cicely Yeovil, whose husband is the main character in the book. The latter, in fact, is Munro's spokesman, and his reaction to the *fait accompli* (i.e., the conquest of Great Britain by William) is one of horrified indignation. He naturally does not share his wife's desire to enjoy café society while his country is

---

12 *Ibid.*, p. 153.
13 *Ibid.*, pp. 157–58.
14 *Ibid.*, p. 256.

enslaved. It is with ill-concealed glee, therefore, that he reads to her (on the morning following the gala event) what the paper, the *Standart*, has to say about Gorla:

> "The wolves which appeared earlier in the evening's entertainment are, the programme assures us, trained entirely by kindness. It would have been a further kindness, at any rate to the audience, if some of the training, which the wolves doubtless do not appreciate at its proper value, had been expended on Miss Mustelford's efforts at stage dancing. We are assured, again on the authority of the programme, that the much-talked-of Suggestion Dances are the last word in Posture dancing. The last word belongs by immemorial right to the sex which Miss Mustelford adorns, and it would be ungallant to seek to deprive her of her privilege. As far as the educational aspect of her performance is concerned we must admit that the life of the fern remains to us a private life still. Miss Mustelford has abandoned her own private life in an unavailing attempt to draw the fern into the gaze of publicity. And so it was with her other suggestions. They suggested many things, but nothing that was announced on the programme. Chiefly they suggested one outstanding reflection, that stage-dancing is not like those advertised breakfast foods that can be served up after three minutes' preparation. Half a lifetime, or rather half a youthtime is a much more satisfactory allowance."[15]

It should be noted that even in this, his most serious work, Saki's gift of happy and unexpected nomenclature is in evidence. And the same may be said of his gift of lighthearted, irresponsible nonsense, as illustrated above.

The sadness and pessimism, however, that we detected in the background of his other works are predominant. Saki's outlook on life cannot be styled a confirmed cynicism, but it does partake of a gravity of outlook that foresees realistically and impatiently the inevitable consequences of folly and self-deception. In *When William Came*, we are reminded of this con-

---

[15] *Ibid.*, p. 222.

stantly, especially in the gloomy forebodings of Yeovil, whose chief complaint against his countrymen is that there are too many patriots and too little patriotism.[16]

Munro's work, in the last analysis, is simply that—a complaint, an indictment of his countrymen. With just humor, he discerningly discriminates between the good and evil tendencies of England's national life. And with well-reasoned logic he reconstructs a hypothetical conquest that was more nearly realized in the second, rather than in the first, world conflict. An especially brilliant touch is the emphasis he puts on the enemy's *Blitzkrieg* tactics, which we had occasion to witness at firsthand in the last decade. Dr. Holham is explaining the tragic train of events to Yeovil, who had been absent in Russia at the time:

> "It started," said the doctor, "with a wholly unimportant disagreement about some frontier business in East Africa; there was a slight attack of nerves in the stock markets, and then the whole thing seemed in a fair way towards being settled. Then the negotiations over the affair began to drag unduly, and there was a further flutter of nervousness in the money world. And then one morning the papers reported a highly menacing speech by one of the German Ministers, and the situation began to look black indeed. 'He will be disavowed,' every one said over here, but in less than twenty-four hours those who knew anything knew that the crisis was on us—only their knowledge came too late. 'War between two civilized and enlightened nations is an impossibility,' one of our leaders of public opinion had declared on the Saturday; by the following Friday the war had indeed become an impossibility, because we could no longer carry it on. It burst on us with calculated suddenness, and we were just not enough, everywhere where the pressure came. Our ships were good against their ships, our seamen were better than their seamen, but our ships were not able to cope with their ships plus their superiority in aircraft. Our trained men were good against their trained men, but they could not be in several places at once, and the enemy could. Our half-trained men and our untrained men could not master the science of war at a mo-

---

[16] *Ibid.,* p. 241.

ment's notice, and a moment's notice was all they got. The enemy were a nation apprenticed in arms, we were not even the idle apprentice: we had not deemed apprenticeship worth our while. There was courage enough running loose in the land, but it was like unharnassed electricity, it controlled no forces, it struck no blows. There was no time for the heroism and the devotion which a drawn-out struggle, however hopeless, can produce; the war was over almost as soon as it had begun. After the reverses which happened with lightning rapidity in the first three days of warfare, the newspapers made no effort to pretend that the situation could be retrieved; editors and public alike recognized that these were blows over the heart, and that it was a matter of moments before we were counted out. One might liken the whole affair to a snap checkmate early in a game of chess; one side had thought out the moves, and brought the requisite pieces into play, the other side was hampered and helpless, with its resources unavailable, its strategy discounted in advance. That, in a nutshell, is the history of the war."[17]

It is also, we might add, an amazing epitome in many respects, not only of the last two wars, but of the unavoidable third one that might substantiate much better than the others Munro's prophecy. There can be little doubt that here Munro drew upon his knowledge of history; his shrewd imaginative portrayal is as much the product of a careful collation of past world conquests as it is of prophetic insight.

Of one thing, however, we can be certain: Munro was sincere in the consecration and dedication of himself to his country's cause—not only with his pen but with his sword and body as well. Lord Charnwood put the case admirably when he wrote:

> Of many who offered and lost their lives in the War—(many too, be it remembered, who offered but did not lose them)—we, their elders, recall that their military service was more than an adventure of gallant youth, or the cheerful acceptance of an inexorable duty; that they did indeed "there offer and present themselves, their souls and bodies, to be a reasonable, holy and lively sacrifice." In no one was this consecration more plain than in Hector Munro,

---

[17] *Ibid.,* pp. 168–69.

as some few comrades remember him in his too short fighting days, and as some friends at home last saw him while he was still impatiently waiting under training in England. In him, as in others, it shone the more brightly because it in a way impaired the simplicity of his demeanor as a normal, ordinary young man. Yet in one way his conduct was singular, as of a man with a special call and that a humble one. He had seen much of the world; the fighting blood in him was hotter than in most men; and he was certainly not lacking in common all-round capacity and self-reliance. In short, his fitness for a commission and its responsibilities was obvious; while he was no longer quite so young as to be callous to hardship and fatigue or at all unappreciative of any of the comparative amenities in an officer's life. But it was of his own choice that he died a Corporal.[18]

In the early morning of November 13, 1916, in a shallow crater near Beaumont-Hamel, Munro was heard to shout, "Put out that bloody cigarette!" They were the last unpredictable words of Saki, whose tragic end was curiously not unlike that of his creation, Comus Bassington. His end as a private soldier, moreover, seems expressive of his position in English letters. For all his skill, his talent, his industry, his fastidious choice of subject and treatment, he was a modest writer, whose ambition was to do well and not to do importantly. And he did all the better for that.

---

[18] *Ibid.,* pp. 148–49.

CHAPTER IV

The Plays and Political Satire

THE LATER works of Hector Hugh Munro must, even in charity, be described as halfhearted and inferior. *The Death-Trap* and *Karl-Ludwig's Window* are extremely short sketches that would have been better as short stories. *The Watched Pot* has possibilities and was performed in Saki's lifetime. Its wit, humor, and somewhat overpolished and altogether too pat and neat dialogue remind us of the comedy of manners as practiced by Goldsmith, Sheridan, Wilde, Maugham, and Coward. But after the first act it becomes boring, and the dramatist fails to sustain our interest. The ending is woefully anticlimactic, and it is not difficult to understand why it has never been revived. *The Westminster Alice* may have been brilliant satire in its own age because of its timeliness, but, like all political squibs, we find today that it has lost much of its pungency and effectiveness. Despite the footnotes, editorial commentary, and the more obvious satiric thrusts, the modern reader will find little to praise in it. J. A. Spender finds it an unqualified success:

> Such things must either succeed perfectly or fail lamentably, and to succeed perfectly meant not merely copying the form but catching the spirit of the inimitably fantastic original . . . Political parodies are generally dead within a few months of their first appearance, but THE WESTMINSTER ALICE is alive and sparkling after twenty-five years. In several of the sections it seems almost of no importance to recover the political allusions.[1]

---

[1] *Novels and Plays*, p. 293.

But we find it somewhat difficult to share such uncritical approval. The spirit of the original Alice is captured quite faithfully, and the drawings enhance the merit of the work immeasurably, but it is doubtful whether Munro's essay at political satire will be remembered as his short stories surely will.

The initial venture of our author into drama, *The Death-Trap,* is set in a Slavic locale and deals with the suicide of the reigning Prince of Kedaria and three of his officers, whom he does not scruple to poison with the same potion he uses to dispatch himself. When the brief dramatic sketch opens, Girnitza, Vontieff, and Shultze—the three officers—are plotting the death of the Prince. They are just about to enter and murder him when his doctor arrives and, in a moment of inspiration, declares that his days are numbered. At this announcement, of course, the officers retire, but the cruel irony of it is that a more careful examination confirms the doctor's wild guess as to the actual state of the Prince. It is then that the Prince decides upon the course of action we have indicated: he summons the officers to drink with him, and dies gloating over his refined Machiavellianism.

Karl-Ludwig's Window is in the same macabre vein and also deals with suicide. It is an infinitely more subtle and artistic work than its immediate predecessor, although it, too, suffers from a forced and strained theatricality. The window—Saki seems to have been fascinated by the fictive potentialities of windows—is used as the focal point of the action, somewhat in the manner in which Tennessee Williams uses certain stage props in his plays to rivet the audience's attention. But Saki, of course, unlike Williams, attaches no symbolic significance to it. It is simply the most prominent object of the set, a kind of tragic heirloom surrounded by an aura of fatality and doom. The terrible associations it has for the Von Jagdstein family is explained by the *Gräfin,* the widow of the man whose enemies compelled him to hurl himself through the window to his death:

GRAF. Yes, this room is certainly full of his associations. There is his portrait, and there is the window from which he was flung down.

BAR. That makes it all the more horrible. I am a man who belongs to a milder age, and it sickens me to think of the brutal deed that was carried through in this room. How his enemies stole in upon him and took him unawares, and how they dragged him screaming to that dreadful window.

GRAF. Not screaming, I hope; cursing and storming, perhaps. I don't think a Von Jagdstein would scream even in a moment like that.

BAR. The bravest man's courage might be turned to water, looking down at death from that horrid window. It makes one's breath go even to look down in safety; one can see the stones of the courtyard fathoms and fathoms below.

GRAF. Let us hope he hadn't time to think about it. It would be the thinking of it that would be so terrible.

BAR. (*with a shudder*). Ah, indeed! I assure you the glimpse down from that window has haunted me ever since I looked.

GRAF. The window is not the only thing in the room that is haunted. They say that whenever one of the family is going to die a violent death that door swings open and shuts again of its own accord. It is supposed to be Karl-Ludwig's ghost coming in.[2]

The characterization is superficial but the tragic hero is sketched more fully than Prince Dimitri of *The Death-Trap*. In describing her son to Baron Rabel, his mother says of Kurt:

GRAF. Kurt has always been the naughty boy of the family, but he made surprisingly little fuss about being betrothed to Isadora. He said he should never marry any one he loved, so it didn't matter whom I married him to. That was at least accommodating.

BAR. That was at least accommodating.

GRAF. Besides the financial advantages of the match the girl's aunt has a very influential position, so for a younger son Kurt is doing rather well.

BAR. He is a clever boy, is he not?

GRAF. He has the perverse kind of cleverness that is infinitely

<hr>

2 *Ibid.,* p. 356.

more troublesome than any amount of stupidity. I prefer a fool like Isadora. You can tell beforehand exactly what she will say or do under any given circumstances, exactly on what days she will have a headache, and exactly how many garments she will send to the wash on Mondays.

BAR. A most convenient temperament.

GRAF. With Kurt one never knows where one is. Now, being in the same regiment with the Archduke ought to be of some advantage to him in his career, if he plays his cards well. But of course he'll do nothing of the sort.

BAR. Perhaps the fact of being betrothed will work a change in him.

GRAF. You are an optimist. Nothing ever changes a perverse disposition. Kurt has always been a jarring element in our family circle, but I don't regard one unsatisfactory son out of three as a bad average. It's usually higher.[3]

Kurt, it appears, is a great deal like Saki's other notoriously unruly sons of the Reginald and Clovis stamp. His tragic fate also places him in close affinity with Comus. Like Comus, Fate precipitates him to an early demise that he accepts as philosophically as it is possible for a man in full bloom of youth to do:

KURT *(quietly)*. I have killed the Archduke.

GRAF. Killed the Archduke! Do you mean you have murdered him?

KURT. Scarcely that: it was a fair duel.

GRAF. *(wringing her hands)*. Killed the Archduke in a duel! What an unheard-of scandal! Oh, we are ruined!

BAR. *(throwing his arms about)*. It is unbelievable! What, in Heaven's name, were the seconds about to let such a thing happen?

KURT *(shortly)*. There were no seconds.

GRAF. No seconds! An irregular duel? Worse and worse! What a scandal! What an appalling scandal!

BAR. But how do you mean—no seconds?

KURT. It was in the highest degree desirable that there should be no seconds, so that if the Archduke fell there would be no wit-

---

[3] *Ibid.*, p. 357.

nesses to know the why and wherefore of the duel. Of course there
will be a scandal, but it will be a sealed scandal.

GRAF. Our poor family! We are ruined.

BAR. *(persistently)*. But *you* are alive. You will have to give
an account of what happened.

KURT. There is only one way in which my account can be rendered.

BAR. *(after staring fixedly at him)*. You mean——?

KURT *(quietly)*. Yes. I escaped arrest only by giving my *parole*
to follow the Archduke into the next world as soon as might be.

GRAF. A suicide in our family! What an appalling affair. People will never stop talking about it.[4]

Saki's clumsy attempts to reveal character through dialogue
here are woefully pathetic and illustrate the often-observed
phenomenon of a fairly proficient literary artist failing dismally
when he abandons his native habitat. Saki would never have
been a dramatist, despite his wit and gift for invention. He was
totally inept in the matter of a long and sustained complication
of plot, and he lacked the faculty of arousing for his characters
anything but a perfunctory interest. The ending to the second of
his one-act plays is the very stuff of cheap melodrama, and one
even seems to catch his sardonic smile as he penned it—half in
earnest and half in jest:

OFFICER. He gave me his word that I should find him here at
nine o'clock, and that I should come too late to arrest him. It seems
he has tricked me!

GRAF. A Von Jagdstein always keeps his word. *(She stares fixedly at the open window. The* OFFICER *follows the direction of her
gaze, goes over to the window, looks out and down. He turns back
to the room, straightens himself and salutes.)*[5]

Averting our petrified glance from the horrific spectacle of
Kurt's suicide, we come to a consideration of *The Watched Pot*,
the most pretentious of Munro's endeavors in the field of dra-

---

4 *Ibid.*, pp. 358–59.
5 *Ibid.*, p. 363.

ma. It is a three-act play whose sole virtue appears to be in its epigrams, of which we have more than the play can easily carry. The central situation is one of light comedy and presents us with the spectacle of a drove of predatory females seeking to ensnare in marital toils the highly eligible bachelor Trevor Bavvel, who is pictured somewhat in the role of Shaw's Jack Tanner. Trevor is the only son of Hortensia Bavvel, a strait-laced widow who rules her household with an absolute tyranny, and takes care to prevent a sudden end to her oligarchy by sedulously guarding against the marriage of her son. Opposed to her views in regard to Trevor's single status are Ludovic Bavvel, Trevor's uncle, who himself smarts under his sister's sovereign sway, and several eligible maidens who ardently wish to terminate their state of freedom via the nuptial route. Among these are Agatha Clifford, Clare Hennessey, Sybil Bomont, and Mrs. Peter Vulpy.

All of the characters are entertaining, although none of them calls forth any real sympathy or, for that matter, genuine interest. Mrs. Bavvel reminds us of Mrs. Bassington in her pertinacious desire to remain head of the family and sole monarch of Briony. We are informed by Munro's sister, in her introduction to the play, that Hortensia is from life, but that the tyranny of her prototype was confined to her own family. She is very much like the formidable and intolerant aunts whom we meet in the author's short stories. The Dean who answered her appeal for material pertaining to the Puritan movement on the back of a postcard admirably gauged her character for us by implication:

> "The Puritan movement was a disease, wholesome though irritating, which was only malignant if its aftereffects were not guarded against."[6]

As might have been expected, Hortensia was not amused,

---

[6] *Ibid.*, p. 382.

and promptly sent off a letter of complaint to the Bishop. Strangely enough, however, she is not used as the main butt of the dramatist's humor, and at the end, her discomfiture is not at all decisive. She faces up to the disclosure of her son's secret marriage quite calmly and entirely unruffled. There is no indication whatever that her reign will be terminated summarily.

Her son Trevor, is comparatively colorless by comparison, and one has difficulty in imagining him as the cynosure of all neighboring, calculatingly possessive female eyes. But then he is an heir of a sort, and surely Saki need not tell us that women place financial security above all else in these matters. His deception in concealing his secret marriage from all concerned, including Agatha and Sybil, who aspired to be his life partner, is in extremely bad taste, not to say hardly credible. What is more, he has too many foppish affectations to please the general public.

The Georgian Amazons are for the most part nonentities, and altogether too tentative in their flirtatious endeavors to make the plot interesting, let alone exciting. Sybil is the most promising of the lot, and we cannot help feel that she is too good for Trevor. Agatha is a wallflower, constantly getting in everybody's way and forever making a nuisance of herself by littering the house with distasteful and atrocious vegetation and flora. Clare is sharp-tongued and the most assured, but then, she had reason to be, since, at the end, we learn she had been secretly wedded to Trevor several months before. Mrs. Vulpy can best be characterized as a "deep one." She knows—so to speak—her way around, and although by no means a *femme fatale,* she is just as deadly. Her refined callousness is strongly in the vein of the affected ennui painstakingly practiced by the women of Restoration comedy. Her character is admirably epitomized for us by Saki in her comment regarding the condition of her husband, who is gravely ill:

"For all I know to the contrary, he may by this time have joined the majority, who are powerless to resent these intrusions, but my private impression is that he's sitting up and taking light nourishment in increasing doses."[7]

A further insight into her character is gained from her conversation with Ludovic, in which the latter solicits her aid in his plan to throw Trevor into the arms of one of the girls:

> LUD. I'm not a wealthy man, but if you help me pull this through I promise you my gratitude shall take concrete shape. A commemorative bracelet, for instance—have you any particular favourite stones?
>
> MRS. V. I love all stones—except garnets or moonstones.
>
> LUD. You think it unlucky to have moonstones?
>
> MRS. V. Oh, distinctly, if you've the chance of getting something more valuable. I adore rubies; they're so sympathetic.[8]

As for the plot itself, we have already remarked that it is rather lumbering and tedious. The surprise ending is, of course, always good theater, but a moment's reflection is sufficient to convince us that, in this instance, it is not only poor craftsmanship but disagreeable as well. We feel we have been tricked in an unfair manner, and we resent it. We are willing to condone such a plot trick in a short story, but we cannot be so indulgent toward Saki in a drama. If Clare and Trevor had been married all along, then it seems unduly cruel to us that they should have trifled with the emotions of their guests—not to say those of the theater audience. Jesting of this kind is well and good, fitting and proper, only when in its own time and place. But the line has to be drawn somewhere. Nor can Saki be excused on the basis that the duped, like the cormorants in Jonson's *Volpone* or the perennial cuckolds in Restoration comedy, were in a sense would-be dupers. We love Falstaff when *he* turns the tables on the Prince and Poins. But we have no relish for the

---

[7] *Ibid.,* p. 366.

[8] *Ibid.,* p. 376.

turners of the tables in Saki. Malice is not always in the best of taste, or good humor. Munro would have done well to have learned this lesson from Pope's *Rape of the Lock.* Had he done so, he might have been a better dramatist, certainly a superior satirist.

But, as always, much can be forgiven Munro by virtue of his sparkling dialogue. We have, for example, the incomparable epigrams and *bon mots* on husbands, wives, and marriage, in the best tradition of the comedy of manners. In a conversation between Sybil and Agatha, we have the following sage remarks on husbands:

> SYBIL. A husband with asthma has all the advantages of a cap-
> tive golf-ball; you always know pretty well where to put your hand
> on him when you want him.
> AGATHA. But if I had a really nice man for a husband I should
> want him to be able to come with me wherever I went.
> SYBIL. A woman who takes her husband about with her every-
> where is like a cat that goes on playing with a mouse long after
> she's killed it.[9]

We cannot help thinking of Wilde's plays again when, warning Stephen Sparrowby off Sybil, whom he has designated for Trevor, Ludovic says:

> "Go fishing in Norway or fall in love with a chorus girl. There
> are heaps of chorus girls who are willing to marry commoners if
> you set the right way about it. But you mustn't think of Sybil Bo-
> mont."[10]

And it is questionable whether Noel Coward himself could improve on René St. Gall's pregnant asseverations on wives:

> "I dislike the idea of wives about a house: they accumulate
> dust . . . Satisfactory wives aren't made: they're invented. Chiefly
> by married men."[11]

---

9 *Ibid.,* p. 376.
10 *Ibid.,* p. 391.
11 *Ibid.,* p. 402.

In clever counterpoint to this we have the women's views on husbands—views that all male aspirants to connubial bliss might well consider before yielding to the impulse of a panic-laden moment:

> CLARE. One can afford to be neglected by one's own husband; it's when other people's husbands neglect one that one begins to talk of matrimonial disillusion.
> MRS. V. Other people's husbands are rather an overrated lot. I prefer unmarried men any day; they've so much more experience.
> CLARE. I don't agree with you. Isn't there a proverb: "A relapsed husband makes the best rake"?
> AGATHA. You're positively disgraceful, both of you. We used to be taught to be content with the Ten Commandments and one husband; nowad ys women get along with fewer commandments and want ten husbands.[12]

Two gems, in particular, even Shaw might have been proud to acknowledge his very own. The speaker in both instances is Ludovic. To Trevor, he confides:

> "Granted that woman is merely a bad habit, she's a habit that we have not grown out of."[13]

—And to the man-rapacious Mrs. Vulpy, he caustically observes:

> "Brevity is the soul of widowhood."[14]

In these delightful verbal delicacies, we have the quintessential Sakian flavor, which is as easy to recognize and as difficult to define as poetry was to Emily Dickinson. It is the prime quality for which we prize Saki in his lighter moments. But it is totally absent when Saki turns to political satire and sets out to laugh away on a billowy gust of hilarity the chicanery and deviousness of British politics. Saki struck good and telling

---

12 *Ibid.,* p. 426.
13 *Ibid.,* p. 439.
14 *Ibid.,* p. 308.

blows at social superstitions, but the old formula and endless array of "types" fail on more serious topics.

The Westminster Alice shows great promise but is altogether too sketchy and fragmentary to merit comparison with other famous English satires. The work falls into thirteen brief sections, and although in several of them it is not necessary to recover the political allusions to appreciate the satire, many are completely meaningless in 1963, even with footnotes.

"Alice in Downing Street" is a cutting assault against Mr. Arthur Balfour, First Lord of the Treasury in Lord Salisbury's third administration (1895–1900). He is pictured as a scrawny penguin and is alluded to as "the Ineptitude." Saki's satire in a sense sums up the public's reaction to the irritating continuance of the Boer War. The public had been thoroughly aroused at the Government's dilatory tactics, its fatal underestimation of the enemy's strength and resourcefulness, and its general "ineptitude." Seeking a scapegoat, they somewhat unjustly fixed on Mr. Balfour, since his superior, Lord Salisbury —pictured quite appropriately by Saki as fast asleep—did a discreet disappearing act during the heated crisis. The section terminates quite abruptly as Alice, the Cat, the enervated King (the Marquess of Salisbury), and the Ineptitude stand puzzled and uncertain while the rambunctious Queen (Mr. Joseph Chamberlain, Secretary of State for the Colonies, 1895–1903), who is adamant in insisting that everyone shall wear khaki, threatens to make her appearance at any moment.

"Alice in Pall Mall" gives us perhaps the most ingenious and striking creation in the whole work—the White Knight (the Marquess of Lansdowne, Secretary of State for War, 1895–1900). In him we find epitomized all those war experts who serenely continue to assure us that there is no threat of war, even while screaming shells are demolishing our cities. When Alice quite naïvely questions him in regard to a war he

is waging in South Africa, inquiring whether he has brought
it to a successful conclusion, he replies:

> "Not exactly to a *conclusion*—not a *definite* conclusion, you
> know—nor entirely successful either. In fact, I believe it's going on
> still . . . But you can't think how much forethought it took to get
> it properly started."[15]

He then goes on to explain to Alice the reason for his obsoles-
cent caparisons and arms:

> ". . . you observe this little short-range gun that I have hanging to
> my saddle? Why do you suppose I sent out guns of that particular
> kind? Because if they happened to fall into the hands of the enemy
> they'd be very little use to him. That was my own invention."
>
> "I see," said Alice gravely; "but supposing you wanted to use
> them against the enemy?"
>
> The Knight looked worried. "I know there is that to be thought
> of, but I didn't choose to be putting dangerous weapons into the
> enemy's hands. And then, again, supposing the Basutos had risen,
> those would have been just the sort of guns to drive them off with.
> Of course they didn't rise; but they might have done so, you
> know."[16]

The Knight's complacent obtuseness is very amusing until the
sober reflection that such men often conduct our fights for freedom and survival darkens the moody frontier of our brows.
Saki is right. There is more stupidity and nearsightedness in
War Ministers than was ever dreamt of in our philosophy.

"Alice and the Liberal Party" good-humoredly satirizes party
factions and politicians with literary pretensions. The Unkhaki
Messenger of the King is Mr. John Morley, who was an active
anti-imperialist and the author of a biography of Oliver Crom-
well. The Primrose Courier is Lord Rosebery, who was the
leader of the Liberal Imperialists and the writer of a work on
Napoleon at St. Helena. Morley had retired from party politics
in 1898; Lord Rosebery had resigned the leadership of the

---

15 *Ibid.,* p. 308.
16 *Ibid.,* p. 308.

Liberal Party in 1896. Saki is poking fun at their sudden reappearance on the political scene in 1900. The trite moral of his satiric sketch reduces to "Once a politician always a politician."

"Alice at Lambeth" is a palpable hit against the squabbles of Protestants and Anglo-Catholics, and hence universally applicable. But compared to *A Tale of a Tub* it strikes one as petty and rather nastily puerile.

"Alice at St. Stephen's" satirizes the hypocritical relationship existing between the Speaker and a member of the House of Commons, a relationship that compels the latter to employ the most extravagant form of circumlocution in his criticisms of his head.

The remaining sections detail the "khaki election" of 1900 and the North-East Lanark by-election in September, 1901. In the latter, Sir W. H. Rattigan secured the seat through a split in the Liberal and radical vote, Mr. Cecil Harmsworth standing as a Liberal Imperialist and Mr. R. Smillie as an Independent Labour candidate. In "Alice in Difficulties," Saki presents Alice in a game of croquet with two flamingos. The balls are live hedgehogs, one of them labeled "Rattigan" and the other "I.L.P." (Independent Labour Party) on one side and "L.I." (Liberal Imperialist) on the other. The flamingos themselves are Sir Edward Grey and Lord Rosebery. The hedgehogs are described as opinionated, shortsighted, and of prickly tempers. The flamingos are equally bad tempered, and eccentric to boot. One of them strays off into a furrow to bore a tunnel. (The "furrow" is an allusion to a speech in which Lord Rosebery had said, "I must plough my furrow alone.") His object in boring a tunnel is to avoid the "cross-currents," i.e., the differences in the Liberal Party.

This general ridicule of the devious conduct and dilatory tactics of politicians is continued in "Alice Anywhere But in Downing Street." In this section Alice pointedly asks the Red Queen and the White Queen why the war is being continued.

But she receives no satisfaction. The White Queen, having re-
course to the theory of relativity and the notion that thinking
so is tantamount to being so, explains to Alice that one has
only to convince one's self that there is no war to terminate
the war. But when pressed further, the Queens either fly to
Christian Science or fall asleep. There then follows a section,
"Alice in a Fog," which ridicules the verses of the Poet
Laureate, Alfred Austin, who had written an ode to greet the
Duke of York, George V subsequently, upon his return from
Australia. And the whole imaginative farce ends as the fol-
lowers of the Red King (Lord Rosebery) rush out *en masse*
to hear him deliver his famous Chesterfield speech (December
16, 1901), which terminated his long period of somnolence.
All the while the bewildered White King is vainly trying to
record Hamlet-like his feelings in a notebook.

These later works of Saki, although of minor value in evaluating the whole of his achievement, nevertheless do afford us
an opportunity to gain a deeper insight into his essential character. For here, surely, the urbane mask of imperturbability is
off, and it is significant that what we find uppermost underneath
it is the earnest critic of society and politics. One also is aware,
not so much that Munro has mellowed, but that he has tired,
that he has written himself out. Many of the epigrams in the
plays are lifted verbatim from the short stories and novels, and
The Westminster Alice not only evinces signs of fitful composition but ends abruptly like a daily cartoon.

But even more important, these later writings of Munro
clarify his concept of irony. On a mature level, irony involves
a conflict in the moral sense: the real versus the ideal. But on
the level of schoolboy humor it may be primitive and savage.
In his short stories, Saki makes a greater use of the latter than
he does of the former. Many of them are nothing but painful
practical jokes. But in his novels, plays, and *The Westminster
Alice* the irony is informed with moral animus. Unlike Swift,

who was impelled to irony by hate or indignation and therefore could feel no pity for his victims, Munro reveals in his irony an intrinsic human kindliness. His sarcasm may be partisan, but it is usually impelled by a heartfelt and genuine intolerance —seldom if ever does he write from pure personal spite. The distinction is a nice one and does not contradict our assertion earlier in this chapter that Saki's humor often reduces to indecorous malice. The malice is there because of an esthetic, not a human, failing. Saki never indulges in the ruthless objectivity of a Voltaire or a Swift.

Conclusion

THERE ARE some authors who elude the scalpel of the Dryas-dusts as exasperatingly as the White Whale, Moby Dick, eluded the passionate pursuit of Captain Ahab. Protean-like they defy the confining nets of the literary scavengers and refuse to lend themselves to any neat critical vivisection. Such a writer was H. H. Munro. Invalided home on the heels of his seventh attack of malaria, and unable to keep bears, a jack-daw, several Persian cats, and a fox terrier at the same time, he took up writing instead. When his first venture dedicated to Clio—*The Rise of the Russian Empire*—was dismissed by critics and historians alike as of little value or merit, he re-solved henceforth to abandon that thankless Muse and pay all his homage to mirth.

It is interesting to speculate whether or not Saki is required reading for Russian diplomats, and what it was that attracted Munro to make a historical study of Russia!

After 1900, Munro devoted himself to journalism and satire. He wrote short stories with the facility with which Byron turned out verse. But unlike Byron, whose poetry is often marred by ungrammatical constructions and awkward syncopations, Munro's prose is as impeccable as the polished couplets of Alexander Pope. He devised his sentences with the same spin-sterish fervor with which Emily Dickinson shaped her flawless lyrics, and chose his words with the same uncanny felicity with which Jane Austen selected her adjectives.

In temper and intention, the greater bulk of Saki's works

are purely comic pieces, distinguished by a crisp, insouciant elegance and easiness of manner, a fertility of invention and sparkling gaiety of dialogue and narrative—the temper and intention of the comedy of manners. They introduce us to a world where nothing is ever solved, nothing altered, a world, in short, extremely like our own, only you are not asked to believe in it. It is the world of a George Meredith or an Oscar Wilde, a world realistic merely in its imaginative resemblance to the world we know—a world that amuses only because we dare not, even for a moment, entertain the thought that our own society harbors the rank hypocrisy, the inhuman sadism, the refined perfidy, the barbarous intolerance, and the moral obtuseness that are part and parcel of Saki's universe.

Saki has many affinities with the Restoration dramatists. Like them he never is explicitly didactic and moralistic. Like Wycherley and Congreve, he frequently even gives the impression that he delights and approves of that brittle and hollow frivolity that inheres in the society he depicts. There are, in fact, many cogent reasons that can be advanced to demonstrate that there was no conscious intent-to-correction in Saki. Our disagreement with this point of view has been presented in the preceding chapters. We have shown that, although Saki cannot lay claim to the title of a Juvenal or a Swift, his works have enough of ridicule and rebuke in them so that we need have no qualms in placing him alongside a Wycherley, an Oscar Wilde, a Charles Dickens, or a Mark Twain. The satiric intent does not predominate to the exclusion of all else in Saki, but no careful reader can be oblivious to the fact that it plays a very prominent part. We cannot subscribe to the claim that his writings serve only to amuse, and nothing else. It is simply not true, for there are many things that Saki has written that do anything *but* amuse. There are many stories that actually revolt and shock the reader. And certainly we cannot be accused of misrepresentation if we read certain of his works as definite attacks on those things that he rebelled against in his society. *The Importance of Being Earnest* was just as damaging an attack on Victorian standards as Butler's *The Way of All Flesh.* In the same way, Saki's works are no less incisive in their criticism of society because they are urbanely ironic and humorous. In the end, horror and laughter are one—when horror and laughter become as horrible and laughable as they can be. This is a lesson Saki teaches us time and again. The weird and the horrible aspects of life held a strange fascination for him, and almost invariably he exploited them for a savage, primitive humor that often verges on nihilism.

To Munro, in fact, life often seemed a sorry joke with no discoverable significance, yet there were occasions when he found in it, as seen in *When William Came,* a certain purposiveness. As he grew older, he was less inclined to distinguish the value of art from the value of life, and readier to perceive in human destiny a beauty and significance that did not derive entirely from the fictitious invention of the artist but were independent and intrinsic. At the end, surely, he was groping his way toward an acceptance of life. Although he died without achieving it, his later writings reveal a human sympathy totally lacking in the early sketches. True (and he was the first to admit it), his works generally point out evil without offering a solution. But what of that? The satirist is a critic of society. Is his function to extirpate evil by drawing our attention to it, or is he required to rectify the abuses he castigates? We would also do well to remember that human nature can never be changed; the most that a satirist can hope to achieve is to laugh away some of the more egregious abuses of the time. To the extent that Swift and Saki tilt against human nature *per se,* to that extent are they engaged in as futile a Herculean labor as any of those undertaken by the devoted knight of Dulcinea del Toboso.

But to the extent that they are justly enraged, to that extent are they the champions of that selfsame mankind that they take to task.

The Merriam-Webster Dictionary defines satire as "a literary composition holding up human or individual vices or foibles, or abuses or shortcomings of any kind, to reprobation by means of ridicule, derision, burlesque, or other method of intensifying incongruities, usually with an intent to provoke amusement." The laughter engendered by satire, however, is not always that of genuine amusement. When satire is inculcated into pure comedy, the robust laugh frequently occasioned by comedy is replaced by a cynical smile. Meredith, for example, is writing satire when he permits us to detect his ridicule, and makes us feel uneasy as a result. Nor are we justified in saying that the habitual reaction to satire is intellectual. For the satirist, like the true moralist, often appeals to the emotions, since satire is frequently moralistic in its intent. In deriding existing follies, the satirist may indirectly be advancing reforms. Satire is an adult ridicule, superseding the childish taunt. It has been called refined invective, and many times degenerates into pure invective. At its best, one may view it as an admission and vehement deprecation of the shortcomings of society. The particular brand of satire employed by Congreve, Gay, Sheridan, and Munro is of this latter type; the rebuke is sprightly and is alleviated by genuine humor. We have criticism but not spite; indignation but not abuse. Munro was capable of hatred, but in his works we find an amused spectator of the "tale told by an idiot," rather than an active participant in the "sound and fury." Yet he was almost—though not absolutely—sure it signified nothing.

"Humor," however, is the important word in any thorough analysis of H. H. Munro. Saki's humor is impish and sardonic. It is as much in the tradition of the classical comedy of ideas as in the tradition of the Dickensian comedy or farce of character. Saki's comic spirit is a dry, impersonal one caught in the clear crystal of delightful witty prose. "Life," says Horace Walpole, "is a comedy to him who thinks, a tragedy to him who feels." That is one reason why Saki seems perhaps a little cruel to so many people, at least upon an initial reading. For Saki's humor is essentially the heedless, almost Nietzschean, nonmoral humor of a child. It is with children especially, in fact, that he is at his best. And this, we have had occasion to observe, is not because his children talk or act like children, but because they think, they react like children. It is in their world we move when we read "The Story-teller" or "The Lumber Room"—a world of make-believe and escape, the world of Peter Pan and Alice. Paradoxes present themselves as reasonably as day and night; it is the grownups, in brief, who are fantastic, and who so helplessly immolate themselves on Saki's ridicule. His children correspond to Swift's Gulliver—they are the means by which Saki puts across his satire.

Therein lies Saki's true forte; he was a past master in telling a fantastic tale with a poker face. Swift, too, told tales with a grave face—"A Modest Proposal"—but as often as not his tale was marred by an embittered misanthropy. Then there is Mark Twain, who also distinguished himself in the narrating of tall tales without blinking an eyelid. But the telling was everything in Mark Twain and the phraseology nothing. Saki's stories resemble those of the American humorist, but his manner in the telling of them puts us more in mind of Max Beerbohm. Saki had the gift of recounting the most fantastic of tales in the most matter-of-fact way.

What is more, his characters fit his plots admirably; they are as fantastic as his narratives. They are not consistent always with life, but they are in perfect keeping with the exotic world of his imagination. His Bertie van Tahns, his Clovis Sangrails —like the Sir Fopling Flutters and Mirabells of Restoration comedy—have an identical imperturbable elegance and ease, a like temper and intention: a characteristic irony displayed toward things of the spirit, a negligent pleasure in things of the flesh. In a word, Saki is one of those few writers who give us double value for our money. For the not overly bright he provides some excellent escapist fare, whereas for the select coterie of those who appreciate high comedy and relish irony, he entertains with his sly digs à la Chaucer and his sardonic reflections.

And for those who crave the unusual and supernatural in their fiction, we have "Sredni Vashtar" and "The Cobweb," wherein Saki achieves an authentic atmosphere of the macabre and horrible akin to the best of Ambrose Bierce. Munro, to be sure, is no Monk Lewis, but his skill in the evocation of the spine-chilling and weird is by no means amateurish. Perhaps the only time we resent his excursions into the eerie is in *The Unbearable Bassington,* where a black dog is introduced just before Comus sails for Africa. Here we feel the unnatural is not only unnecessary but theatrical as well, whereas in "Sredni" it is completely sinister and hence very effective.

Even tragedy is not beyond his versatile powers, as we saw in the first of his novels. Comus is dying in a small river village in deepest Africa, and the loneliness, the sense of exile, he feels as he watches the old and yet familiar, trivial scene that Saki conveys is simply done and, perhaps for that very reason, infinitely touching, tragic:

> Comus sat and watched it all with a sense of growing aching depression. It was so trivial to his eyes, so devoid of interest, and yet it was so real, so serious, so implacable in its continuity, the brain grew tired with the thought of its unceasing reproduction. It had all gone on, as it was going on now, by the side of the great rushing, swirling river, this tilling and planting and harvesting, marketing and store-keeping, feast-making and fetish-worship and love-making, burying and giving in marriage, child-bearing and child-rearing, all this had been going on, in the shimmering, blistering heat, and the warm nights, while he had been a youngster at school, dimly recognizing Africa as a division of the earth's surface

that it was advisable to have a certain nodding acquaintance with. It had been going on in all its trifling detail, all its serious intensity, when his father and his grandfather in their day had been little boys at school, it would go on just as intently as the shadows would lengthen and fade under the mulberry trees in that far-away English garden, round the old stone fountain where a leaden otter forever preyed on a leaden salmon.[1]

But there can be little doubt that it is his stories rather than his novels that will be read. His aphoristic style becomes a little trying in a full-length novel, and his wittiness begins to cloy the appetite when overly prolonged. After all, Saki is, indeed, caviare to the general, and although we prize the delectable repast of sturgeons' eggs as the crowning glory of a succulent supper, we do not crave them as a staple course on the daily menu. Many of his stories, it must be admitted, were merely occasional journalism distinguished by a sparkling originality and animation, a pristine freshness that was peculiarly his own, but it is those qualities exactly that make all the difference. The elegant Junior League set of prewar days is as deftly caricatured by Saki as are the Victorian rogues and saints by Dickens. No other writer has ever held up to ridicule the decorous amenities of an English week-end party on such rollicking gales of withering laughter. No other writer has portrayed with more consummate irony the hypocrisy and envenomed conversation of ladies at bridge.

In conclusion, we can only say that Saki deserves a great deal more critical recognition and reading than many humorists whose most trivial obiter dicta are treasured by everybody as so much revelation. But there is one particular in which we beg to differ from the rabid devotees of his works. It is, alas, the tragedy of many young men to have died prematurely before their work was done or even started; it is the tragedy of many more to have survived. We feel Saki had probably said

---

[1] H. H. Munro, *Novels and Plays of Saki* (London, 1945), pp. 132–33.

everything he had to say; he had selected an artificial and brilliant and flippant philosophy, for all his profound understanding of human nature, and while he was interesting and important for his potentialities, it is doubtful whether he would have gone any further. After all, he made some delightful contributions to contemporary letters; he was never dull—and that is more than can be said for most modern comic writers—and he has given us a comic world that we would not willingly let die. Saki did not see life whole, but he did see it steadily; his ironic vision saw to that.

Letters of Miss Ethel M. Munro to the Author

[Penwritten]

75 Goldhurst Terrace
Hampstead
London N.W. 6
19 July 1952

DEAR MR. SPEARS,

I am writing to you at once in answer to yours received to day, to say that I had many letters of Saki's which are being used by an author who is publishing a life of my brother very soon, and some sketches also, for Saki was an artist as well as a writer. So I have nothing for you. I would write my biography [of Saki] to day exactly the same, without any changes. I have been having a correspondence in "the Spectator" concerning the delusion some English writers have had (only recently though), that he had a "miserable childhood," which is exactly the opposite case; he and his brother and I managed to have a happy and often a very amusing childhood. No one has edited his writings, as far as I know.

Yours sincerely
[Signed] ETHEL M. MUNRO

[*Penwritten*]

11 Aug.
75 Goldhurst Terrace, London, N.W. 6

My letters in "Spectator" were on June 13, and June 27. S's humour was satirical often, but not "sardonic." It interests me to hear the different points of view on his writing.

Yours sincerely
[*Signed*] E. M. MUNRO

[*Penwritten*]

75 Goldhurst Terrace
London N.W. 6
19 August 1952

DEAR MR. SPEARS

Saki's writing contemporaries had no influence on his style, which was unique, nor on his subject matter. If you read his "Rise of the Russian Empire" you will see that it is different from his usual style, as the author writing his biography has found. I believe the book is now out of print.

He spoke Russian fluently but am not sure if he read it so well. He lived so long ago, that it is difficult to remember details.

One subject he never wrote on, was sex, and I am certain if he had, he would have made fun of it. The best way to treat it!

Yours sincerely
[*Signed*] E. M. MUNRO

[*Penwritten*]

75 Goldhurst Terrace
  London N.W. 6
   4 Sept. 52

DEAR MR. SPEARS

I think Saki's favourite reading was history, Flecker's "Golden Journey to Samarkand," Russian books, tales of Werwolves, anything weird. When his biography comes out, by Norman Denny, it will be interesting to see what he makes of his life. I am thankful that Saki did not live to be old; he hated the thought of old age and what he went through in the war, might have left him delicate or an invalid. I hope your thesis will be a success.

Best wishes

Yours sincerely
[*Signed*] E. M. MUNRO

Of course he was a Highlander, to his finger tips. Thank you for asking if you could perform any service for me in America, there is nothing, thank you.

Bibliography

PRIMARY SOURCES

Munro, Hector Hugh. *The Best of Saki.* Guild Books #423. London: The Bodley Head, 1950, xi, 179 pp.

A paper-covered popular edition of the better-known short stories. The introduction by Graham Greene, with its charge of an unhappy childhood for Saki, has drawn fire from Miss Ethel Munro. (See Appendix.)

———. *The Complete Works of "Saki"* in eight uniform volumes. London: The Bodley Head, various dates.

v. 1. *The Unbearable Bassington,* Introduction by Maurice Baring, c. 1912, xi, 314 pp.

v. 2. *When William Came,* Introduction by Lord Charnwood, c. 1913, 322 pp.

v. 3. *The Westminster Alice,* Introduction by J. A. Spender, c. 1927, 161 pp.

v. 4. *Reginald and Reginald in Russia,* Introduction by Hugh Walpole, c. 1921, 216 pp.

v. 5. *The Chronicles of Clovis,* Introduction by A. A. Milne, c. 1911, 302 pp.

v. 6. *Beasts and Super-Beasts,* Introduction by H. W. Nevinson, c. 1926, 268 pp.

v. 7. *The Toys of Peace,* Introduction by G. K. Chesterton, c. 1919, 260 pp.

v. 8. *The Square Egg,* with a biography of "Saki" by Ethel M. Munro, c. 1924, 332 pp.

These volumes, published through the years, are now out of print. "Uniform volumes" is a misnomer.

———. "The Miracle-Merchant," in Alice Gerstenberg, editor, *One-Act Plays for Stage and Study,* 8th series. New York: Samuel French, 1934, pp. 345–56.

The only published copy of this one-act farce involving an unwanted guest and hijinks in an English country house. The anthology is used in high schools throughout the United States.

————. *The Novels and Plays of Saki,* complete omnibus edition. New York: Viking Press, c. 1933, 452 pp.

The American counterpart of The Bodley Head edition; except for pagination and typography an exact one.

————. *The Novels and Plays of Saki,* complete in one volume. London: The Bodley Head, 1949, 452 pp.

"The Miracle-Merchant" is absent from this so-called complete edition of the plays. The introduction by Maurice Baring stresses Saki's vein of macabre, supernatural fantasy. Used for footnotes in this study.

————. *Rise of the Russian Empire.* London: Grant Richards, 1900, xii, 344 pp.

Written in an entirely different style from that of his stories and plays, this unscholarly study is the fruit of his years in Russia as a correspondent. It received mediocre reviews. Saki's only serious work.

————. *The Short Stories of Saki.* Complete in one volume. New York: Viking Press, c. 1930, xiii, 718 pp.

The popular American edition. A counterpart of The Bodley Head edition, except for the typography.

————. *The Short Stories of Saki.* London: The Bodley Head, 1949, 720 pp.

The definitive British edition of the short stories and the short biography by Saki's sister, Ethel Munro. The Introduction by Christopher Morley is most laudatory. Used for footnotes in this study.

————. *When William Came.* London: The Bodley Head, 1914, 322 pp.

Printed early in the first year of World War I, this imaginary novel on the Hohenzollern occupation of England proved most un-funny for the same reason Chaplin's film *The Great Dictator* failed—the danger was too close.

GENERAL WORKS

Alden, Raymond M. *Rise of Formal Satire in England Under Classical Influences.* Philadelphia: University of Pennsylvania Press, 1899, vii, 264 pp.

A scholarly monograph on the history of satire in English long considered a definitive work on the subject.

Bergson, Henri. *Laughter: An Essay on the Meaning of the Comic.* New York: Macmillan, 1911, vii, 200 pp.

A serious study of comedy; standard.

Diffenbauch, Guy Linton. *The Rise and Development of the Mock Heroic Poem in England from 1660 to 1714.* Urbana, Illinois, 1926 (University of Illinois thesis for Ph.D.), 280 pp.

Valuable only for a brief analysis of the essence of "mock."

Duffy, Charles, and Henry Pettit, *A Dictionary of Literary Terms.* Denver: University Press, c. 1951, viii, 133 pp.

Fowler, H. W. *Dictionary of Modern English Usage.* Oxford: Clarendon Press, 1926, viii, 742 pp.

A standard reference tool for literary definitions.

Eastman, Max. *Enjoyment of Laughter.* New York: Simon & Schuster, 1936, xviii, 367 pp.

A descriptive study of the psychology of humor and laughter containing many well-chosen examples, illustrated. Too much attention to "gags," but learned and serious much of the time.

Freud, Sigmund. *Wit and Its Relation to the Unconscious.* New York: Moffat, 1917, vii, 21 pp.

Useful for a study of Saki's aunt complex.

Johnson, Edgar. *A Treasury of Satire.* New York: Simon & Schuster, 1945, xxiv, 770 pp.

A superior anthology of the various types of satire edited with a historical background for each. Deplores attempts to analyze Saki.

Kitchin, George. *A Survey of Burlesque and Parody in English.* London: Oliver & Boyd, 1931, xxiii, 387 pp.

A critical history rather than a survey. Repetitive and wordy. Particularly good on difference between parody and imitation.

Leacock, Stephen. *Humor and Humanity: An Introduction to the Study of Humor.* New York: Holt, 1938, 3, 232 pp.

An army of jokes, one after the other, is a cheerless thing. Admirable criticism of humor, English *v.* American.

Mawer, Irene. *The Art of Mime.* London: Methuen, 1932, xii, 244 pp.

Scholarly, uninspired. Used to assist in evaluating the plays. Saki was much interested in mime.

Repplier, Agnes. *In Pursuit of Laughter.* Boston: Houghton Mifflin, 1936, 3, 229 pp.

Traces the history of humor from the Middle Ages. Used in attempting to understand Munro's odd sense of humor.

Sedgewick, G. G. *Of Irony Especially in Drama.* Toronto: University Press, 1948, 100 pp.

One of the Alexander lectures at the University of Toronto. Scholarly and technical.

Thompson, Alan Reynolds. *The Dry-Mock: A Study of Irony in Drama,* Berkeley and Los Angeles: University of California Press, 1948, xviii, 142 pp.

A provocative study of the serio-comic dramatist. Appraises dramatists from point of view of their ironic capabilities. Great range, hence useful in classifying Saki.

Thomson, J. A. K. *Satire and Epigram in Classical Influences on English Poetry.* London: Allen Unwin, 1951, pp. 196–246.

A study of classical influence on the satire in English. Useful in tracing Horatian influence on Munro from his possible readings in great English satires.

Wolfe, Humbert. *Notes on English Verse Satire.* New York: Harcourt Brace, 1929, 158 pp.

One of the Hogarth lectures. Elaborate and metaphorical survey of satire in poetry. Useful for this study in its discussion of the later Victorians and Georgians.

Worcester, David. *The Art of Satire.* Cambridge, Massachusetts: Harvard Press, 1940, ii, 191 pp.

Intelligent and shrewd study of satiric distinctions. Most useful.

Yelland, H. L., S. C. Jones, and K. S. W. Easton, *Handbook of Literary Terms.* New York: Philosophical Library, 1950, 221 pp.

A simple, precise and well-illustrated alphabetical compilation and explanation of literary terms for the use of students.

REVIEWS

"Beasts and Super-Beasts." *Bookmarket,* London, Vol. 46 (August, 1914), p. 225.

Hartley, L. P., "Collected Works of Saki" (review). *Bookmarket,* London, Vol. 71 (January, 1927), pp. 214–17.

Munro, H. H., and Charles Maude. "Watched Pot." Criticism, *Spectator,* Vol. 171, p. 194.

"Rise of the Russian Empire," *Atheneum,* 1900, Vol. 1 (March, 1931), p. 398; *Dial,* Vol. 29 (November 1, 1900), p. 310; *Nation,* Vol. 72 (March 7, 1901), p. 201; *Amer. Hist. Review,* Vol. 7, (Oct., 1901), pp. 138–40.

"Toys of Peace." *Bookmarket,* London, Vol. 56 (April, 1919), pp. 20–21.

ARTICLES

Drew, Elizabeth. "Saki," in the *Atlantic Monthly,* Vol. 166 (July, 1940), pp. 96–98.

Gould, G. "Saki," in the *New Statesman,* Vol. 10, pp. 159–60.

Koppe, E. O. "Portrait," in *Publishers Weekly,* Vol. 118 (October 4, 1930), p. 1621.

Mais, S. P. B. "The Humour of Saki," in *Books and Their Writers.* New York: Dodd, Mead, 1920, pp. 311–30.

Milne, A. A. "Introducing Saki," in *By Way of Introduction.* New York: Dutton, 1929, pp. 28–32.

Morley, Christopher. "Saki," in *Internal Revenue.* New York: Doubleday, Doran, 1933, pp. 223–26.

"Munro, H. H., Biographical Note." *Scholastic,* Vol. 37 (October 14, 1940), p. 30.

"Munro, Hector Hugh (Saki, Pseud.). Portrait," in *Saturday Review of Literature,* Vol. 4 (October 1, 1927), p. 147.

"Munro, H. H., Posthumous Success," in *Publishers Weekly,* Vol. 119 (January 10, 1931), p. 23.

Porterfield, A. "Saki," in *London Mercury,* Vol. 12 (August, 1925) pp. 385–95.

The Satire of Saki

A Study of the Satiric Art of

Hector H. Munro by

GEORGE J. SPEARS

WHEN World War I ended the career of Hector H. Munro, there were many who mourned in the literary world. H. H. Munro, or Saki, as he was known to his reading public, had practiced the art of Swift and Pope and Juvenal with mordant wit and flair.

Born in Burma of English parents, Saki was a comparatively young man when he died, but he was already the author of several plays and novels as well as his famous collections of short stories —generally considered to be his highest achievement.

In this study, the first of its kind, George Spears quoting liberally, considers each of Saki's works in turn, in relation to the nature of its humor and the means Saki employed to achieve his purpose, and in relation to the satiric writing of others.

The Chronicles of Clovis (1911), which Dean Spears considers to be Saki at his best, reveals his understanding and love of animals, his almost inhuman aloofness from suffering, his aptness at satirical nomenclature, his gift for epigram and irony, his penchant for practical jokes and his fascination with the eerie and bizarre.

Saki's best-known protagonists, Clovis and Reginald, are characters without consciences. Their function is a negative one, pricking the pomposity of Saki's